What

d
Comes Around

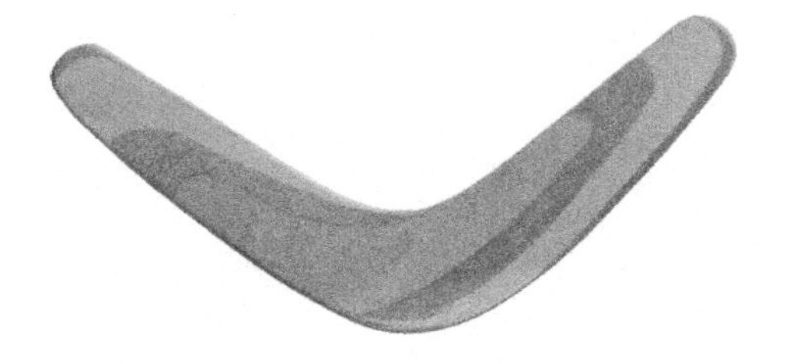

AND OTHER REFLECTIONS

TIM KELLOGG

Printed in the United States by Kindle Direct Publishing.

ISBN: 978-0-578-92183-9

About the Book

This book was written by a father to his adult children for the purpose of sharing reflections of his life experiences. He hopes they will benefit all who read them. Vignettes include: adventures while growing up in a small town, competing in the sport of wrestling, people you meet while hitchhiking and the challenges and joys of raising a family.

The stories in this book are based on real events; however, most of the names have been changed to protect the individuals' privacy.

Author's Goal for this Book

To have the reader smile after reading these stories.

Dedication

To my wife, Lori, for her loving support and encouragement while editing this book.

To Katie, Tyler, Alexa, and Shoshi, each of you have been an inspiration to me as you have taken on new challenges and followed your dreams.

Book cover by Nizar Krayem.

Editing by Cathy Dausman.

Table of Contents

Fearless

I was in second grade when my parents decided our two-bedroom bungalow was too small for the five of us and our Collie so they purchased a larger home on the other side of town. The new house had previously been divided into rental units and was left empty for over a year. Consequently, it required a lot of work before we could move into it. My siblings and I spent every weekend for the next couple of months going with our parents to the new house and getting in the way as they worked to clean, repair and paint it. This was during the winter months and I hadn't met any friends yet in the new neighborhood. One Sunday, I decided to walk back to our old neighborhood to play with my friends. However, it didn't occur to me that I should inform my parents. Also, I'll note that our other house was over two miles away and I was only eight years old at the time; hence, I was undertaking somewhat of a perilous journey. Lucky for me, I had barely left the backyard when my older sister Carol realized I was missing and came looking for me. She caught up with me just as I was about to cross Capital Avenue which carried extremely heavy traffic. I have to say there is nothing more embarrassing for a boy than to have his older sister throw him to the ground, sit on his chest and refuse to let him up until he agrees to her terms. Those terms being an agreement to not cross a busy street. My sister and I began to have a shouting match while she sat on my chest.

Me: “Get off me!”

Carol: “Are you going to cross that street?”

Me: “Yes!”

Carol: “Then I’m not letting you up!”

Me: “Get off me!”

Carol: “No!”

It just so happened we were on the property of a local church and their Sunday morning service was letting out. Seeing and hearing the spectacle that Carol and I were making, the church’s reverend walked over and demanded we leave the church property immediately. Carol, being only twelve years old, turned and looked up at the reverend who towered over both of us. She began speaking softly and slowly as you would expect from a small girl, “I’ll let him up” — but then Carol raised her arm and pointed at the traffic flying past us in the busy street and her voice changed to a lion’s roar as she finished her sentence — “WHEN HE AGREES TO NOT CROSS THAT STREET!”

Realizing he had met his match, the reverend abruptly turned and walked away. At about this time my parents and brother drove up. Upon seeing them, Carol released me so we could get in the car.

Mom and Dad must have decided they didn't need to work on the new house anymore that day because we drove back to our old house where I played with my friends.

I'll never forget Carol's fearless stance against the reverend who had towered over both of us and demanded we leave his church property and how she refused to yield. I was very fortunate to have such a courageous sister.

Many years later I realized the crucial lesson I learned that day: Sometimes it's in one's own best interest not to obtain what one desires. If my sister hadn't stopped me from crossing that busy street, I might not be here today writing this story.

Patience

I used to walk home for lunch every school day during the years that I attended elementary school. These lunch hours were a special time for me because my older brother and sister were in junior high school and they didn't get to come home for lunch; thus, I had my mom's full attention. The typical lunch hour was spent eating and reading with her or working on homework which was due that afternoon. One particular lunch hour stands out in my memory. I had a math assignment due which consisted of adding mixed fractions like $2\frac{1}{7} + 4\frac{3}{5}$. Unfortunately, I was having a challenge grasping the algorithm for solving these types of problems even after my mom had explained it a couple of times. With time running out I asked her to just tell me how to solve each problem. I promised her when I came home that evening, I would figure out how to solve all of the problems on my own. She agreed and began explaining the next problem slowly describing each step. To my surprise, half way through her explanation it became obvious how to solve the problem and I responded, "Wait a minute. I think I got it." I ended up solving it and the rest of the problems on my own.

Sometimes an individual just needs a little extra patience from a person who is willing take the time to explain how to solve a problem or perform a task. I've often thought of that day when I was helping my kids with their homework or assisting a co-worker who was learning how to run a software application. Every now and then it takes more than one explanation for a person to grasp a new concept or skill and I should give it patiently.

Knights and Dragons

One Sunday afternoon my friend Joe and I watched a movie on TV called *The Black Shield of Falworth*. The movie was about medieval knights and we loved it. After the movie ended, we went down into Joe's basement and scavenged two, long, thin pieces of wood to use as swords. Painfully, within only a few minutes of sword fighting, both of us had acquired numerous welts all over our bodies which caused us to realize the need for some type of armor to protect ourselves from ourselves.

We combed through the basement again and found two broken chairs that were destined for the city dump. Joe pulled the cushion off one of the seats and there laid a piece of plywood which could be used to make the perfect sized shield for a 5th grader. All we needed was a pair of handles to attach to the back of each piece of plywood. I then remembered my dad had recently purchased a new pair of leather boots and had thrown his old boots into the trash can. After retrieving the discarded boots, we used a razor knife to cut four leather strips. Next, we nailed two strips onto the back of each piece of plywood. Each pair of leather strips allowed a hand to be threaded through the first strip and then grasp the second strip while leaving the other hand free to wield a sword. We commenced to have a wild sword fight while protecting our bodies with the shields. Not surprisingly, we were making such a racket that Joe's mom (Robin) came downstairs to check on us. Upon seeing the homemade shields, Robin offered to paint a dragon on each one. Both Joe and I immediately agreed to her offer by shouting, "Yes! Yes!"

The following day I ran home from school to see how the dragons looked on the shields. Robin hadn't painted just any old dragons; instead, she painted the fiercest, fire-breathing dragons I had ever seen. Each green dragon was hunched up on its hind legs with its wings fully expanded and a blaze of red flame was streaming out of its mouth. They were absolutely magnificent! I thanked Robin for painting a dragon on my shield then Joe and I ran off to storm some imaginary castles.

Many years later I was reminiscing about my shield and its dragon when I realized what a wonderful gift Robin had given me considering how busy she had been raising her kids and running a household. Later that year, I sent a Christmas card that included a thank you note for the dragon which she had painted on my shield so many years ago. I heard through Joe that the letter was well received.

What might seem like a small gesture to an adult may have a lasting impression on a child such that he or she will remember it decades later.

The Outsiders

During my sixth-grade year in elementary school, I decided to try out for the school's hockey team which played its games on a gymnasium floor as opposed to an ice rink. Unfortunately, when I asked my teacher, who managed the community's hockey program, if I could try out for the school's team, he responded that the team had already been selected from the boys who had played during the previous season. However, he did offer an alternative. If I could recruit eleven other boys to create another team and find a parent to coach us, he would enlist a sponsor to pay our league fee.

This seemed like a reasonable solution so that night I asked my friend Joe if he wanted to play on a hockey team with me. He accepted the offer and we began to debate who should be our coach. We immediately eliminated both of our fathers. Joe's father was a business manager and traveled quite often for his work so he wouldn't have time to coach a team and my dad had a 90-mile commute to work each day; thus, he wouldn't be available to coach us. I then proposed Mr. Roberts, who was a father that lived in the neighborhood. Joe immediately agreed to my suggestion. I'm not sure why we were set on Mr. Roberts coaching us. We didn't know if he had ever played hockey or any other sport. In fact, the only athletic aspect we knew about him was that he rode his bike to work every day during the summer months.

That night we walked over to Mr. Roberts' house and knocked on his door. When he answered, I explained how Joe and I were organizing a new hockey team and I asked him to be our coach. Not surprisingly, Mr. Roberts appeared perplexed and replied that not only had he never played hockey, but he knew very little about the sport. We told him that was okay because neither of us had ever played hockey either and we could all learn together. He paused for a moment and then asked, "How many games are in the season and where are they played?"

Me: "There are eight games and we will play every Saturday at the local Youth building, but we also need to find a place to practice during the week."

Mr. Roberts: "How many boys are on your team?"

Me: "Just Joe and myself, but I'm going to recruit ten more boys to join us."

After replying to Mr. Roberts' last question, I remember a grin creeping across his face. Looking back now I imagine he was asking himself, "Can these two sixth graders get ten additional boys to join their team when neither of them have ever played hockey?" Nonetheless, he replied, "I'll tell you what boys, you round-up your ten additional players and I'll consider your offer." We agreed and left.

The next morning, I started recruiting the rest of our team. However, since all of our school's star athletes were already playing on either the other hockey team or basketball team, I had to recruit boys that not only had never played hockey, but in many cases, had never played in any organized sport. This did not deter me and I started recruiting by first looking for Juan who was an excellent athlete which he demonstrated every day during gym class. The interesting point about Juan was that he had never played on any of our school's teams and I figured it was worth a shot to ask him to join our team. When I spotted him on the playground, I called out, "Hey Juan, how's it going?"

Juan: "It's going well Tim. How about with you?

Me: "Pretty good! I have a question for you.

Juan: "Shoot."

Me: "I've noticed during gym class that you are one of the best athletes in the school."

Juan: "Thanks Tim! I appreciate you saying that."

Me: "So why haven't you ever joined any of the school's sports teams?"

Juan: "I don't know. Maybe because no one ever asked me."

Me: "Well I'm putting together a second hockey team for our school. Will you play on it?"

Juan: “Sure! Who is going to be the coach?”

Me: “His name is Mr. Roberts and he lives near me.”

Juan: “How much does he know about hockey?”

Me: “As much as you and me put together.”

Juan: “That little?”

Me: “Yup!”

Juan: “How much does it cost?”

Me: “It’s free. We are getting a sponsor to pay our league fee.”

Juan: “Can my brother José play on the team?”

Me: “Absolutely!”

Juan: “Cool! I’ll let him know that he has joined the team.

Me: “Excellent!”

And with each boy I asked to play on our hockey team, the answer was, “Yes.” They all wanted to play, but they were outsiders to sports because they had no experience and they just needed to have someone encourage them. For example, Gus was an over-weight boy; however, he had a heart of gold and he worked harder than any of us during practice. Mark was a quiet kid that faded into the crowd, but he was a very dependable player. Hal had just moved to the area and he didn’t know anyone so he was anxious to belong.

Another one of the boys had dyslexia and it made reading extremely challenging. Yet it didn't stop him from being our star player during several games.

Two days later, Joe and I were back on Mr. Roberts' porch updating him with our team roster which included not twelve boys, but fourteen! He must have been contemplating our offer because he promptly agreed to coach our team as well as to speak to the school principal and arrange for us to practice in the school gymnasium.

Disastrously, we were only into our second practice when Mr. Roberts realized he had a serious problem. Only half of our players were showing up for practice. This wasn't too surprising considering most of the boys had never played hockey or any other organized sport. Hence, they weren't accustomed to the idea of attending a weekly practice. To address this challenge, Mr. Roberts leveraged a skill that neither Joe nor I had considered as an asset for being a hockey coach, a pilot's license. At the end of practice, he announced that every player who attended practice regularly and was present for all of the games would receive a free airplane ride at the end of the season. This was an extraordinary offer because none of us had ever flown in an airplane. The offer worked! From that point forward, all of our teammates attended every practice.

I still remember how Mr. Roberts came to practice each Monday evening with new hockey techniques he had studied during the previous weekend and how he would have us drill those techniques over and over until we mastered each one. When practice ended, Mr. Roberts would load up his car with as many boys as possible and give them a ride home so they wouldn't have to walk in the cold, blustery, winter weather.

I have to be honest. This story didn't end like your typical movie. We didn't win the league championship; although, we did win half of our games which we deemed a success considering the inexperience of our players. Also, Mr. Roberts held true to his promise. Three weeks after the hockey season ended, he met all of us boys at the local airport on a Saturday afternoon where he rented a small Cessna. He then took three boys at a time up in the plane and as each flight flew over the streets where the boys lived, Mr. Roberts tipped the plane up on its side so the boys could look down and clearly see their homes. It was a memorable experience for all of us.

I ended up going to both junior high and high school with those boys and that hockey team was the only time most of them ever participated in an organized sport. This experience not only taught each of us how to play as a member of a team, but by following the expectation of attending practices and being present for all games, it taught us the importance of commitment and reliability that would be a benefit in life. Also, it gave us our first airplane ride, free of charge. All of this was possible because a man agreed to coach a neighborhood hockey team, which didn't even exist when we first approached him. We were very fortunate to have had Mr. Roberts as our coach and by observing his commitment to our team, I gained the highest respect for other parents who volunteer to coach kids' teams.

Which Friend Can You Count On?

As I mentioned in the *Fearless* story, I moved to another neighborhood when I was eight. The elementary school in this new area was located next to the hospital so several of the doctors resided nearby allowing them to be readily available in case of emergencies. I ended up attending school with many of their kids, as well as the mayor's son. At the time I was unaware of it, but looking back I now realize there were very few under-privileged kids in my school.

There was one boy who stands out in my memory. His name was Dwayne. He lived on the outskirts of the school district near a poorer section of town and he didn't have the same advantages as either the mayor's or doctors' sons, but at his core, Dwayne was a good kid. I was friendly with Dwayne and we would chat on the playground. Sadly, as with most kids at that age, if you weren't part of the in-crowd, you tended to get teased and Dwayne was definitely teased.

The social dynamics for the kids in my class changed dramatically when we went to junior high school where we were merged with kids from several other elementary schools. These new kids included some excellent athletes who demonstrated their skills every day during gym class when we played flag football in the fall, basketball in the winter and softball in the spring. The school's outside playground was on the opposite side of McCamly Street which was a main street that carried heavy traffic into downtown. For the students' safety, the city built a tunnel beneath the street to allow safe passage to and from the playground. Unfortunately, the city officials didn't take into account that this poorly lit tunnel was the ideal place for fights to take place, especially after playing with a team that had sore losers. With the gym teacher leading the students back through the tunnel, you didn't want to get caught at the end of the line. That was a lesson I learned well one day.

After playing a game of flag football, I was walking with a couple of classmates towards the end of the line when I felt a sharp rap across the back of my head. As I turned around, I found Billy glaring at me. Billy's team had lost their game that day and he had performed poorly. It didn't matter that I had played in a different game. What mattered was that Billy had lost some of his self-respect and he needed to regain it by picking a fight with someone. He always picked a boy smaller than himself. He was a classic bully and I never saw him fight anyone his size. As I squared off to face Billy, who was quite a bit bigger than I, who do you think stepped in between us? It wasn't the mayor's son nor any of the doctors' sons and it wasn't one of my best friends. It was Dwayne who only said three words. It wasn't Dwayne's words that caught Billy's attention, but how he said them with a slow growl and a pause between each word: "Leave…him…alone!" Billy immediately turned and ran forward through the tunnel to the locker room. When I thanked Dwayne for his help, he shrugged his shoulders and nonchalantly said, "No problem." As we continued our walk to the locker room, we talked about the day's game and who had played well.

It's ironic to think who may come to your aid in time of need. It's not always your best friend; sometimes it's a person you hardly know, but one who you treated with respect each day.

Since that day I've made an extra effort to be kind not only to my close friends, but to everyone I meet, especially those individuals who don't seem to have many friends.

A Boy's Best Friend

I was two years old when my parents purchased Ginger, a Collie puppy. For the next ten years Ginger watched over my brother, sister and me as we traipsed about our neighborhood. Years later my mom would tell a story that happened when I was three. Ginger was outside when she began barking incessantly. That was unusual. When Mom went to the front door to check on the commotion, she found I had slipped out of the house and was in the street. At that point, Ginger bit the seat of my pants and pulled me out of harm's way.

Ginger was one smart dog. She shepherded my siblings and me wherever we traveled, especially during the hot summer months when our parents often took us to a nearby lake for a swim. Arriving at the lake's parking lot, my siblings and I would dash ahead of our parents with Ginger running beside us. When we reached the lake, Ginger refused to allow us to enter the water by blocking us with her body while barking constantly until our parents caught up. Only then would Ginger allow us to enter the lake. She was a wonderful guardian, but unfortunately, she passed away the summer before my thirteenth birthday and I was heartbroken.

A few months later on a cold rainy day in October a friend found a huge dog which appeared to be a mix of St. Bernard and Collie. Her mom refused to allow the dog into their house so she brought him over to mine. We gave the dog some food and a warm place to lie down. He didn't have a dog tag or an ID chip; consequently, there was no way for us to contact his owner and he ended up staying with us. Because he weighed over 80 pounds, I felt he deserved a name that demanded respect. I convinced my family to name him Caesar and my dad purchased a collar with a dog tag that included Caesar's name along with our name, address and phone number.

I spent the following winter playing with Caesar in the snow. He was so strong that I could tie my sled onto his collar and he would pull me around the yard. I would also take him on long walks in the neighborhood. During some of these walks, Caesar would break free and run off to chase other dogs, squirrels or birds and sometimes I would lose sight of him. Luckily, within a few hours we would receive a call from either a neighbor or a stranger informing us that he had caught our dog. Taking a leash, I would fetch Caesar and bring him home.

The following Mother's Day, when I came downstairs in the morning, my mom mentioned that Caesar had slipped out through the backyard gate which had been left ajar. Because Caesar had his dog tag on his collar, I assumed someone would catch him and call us just like all the other times when he had slipped away. Sadly, the call never came and I never saw Caesar again.

It was many years later when I came to understand that I really never owned Caesar. Instead, fate had loaned him to me, thereby helping me overcome my grief for the loss of Ginger. Once Caesar's mission was accomplished, he was free to go back to his original owner or on to another person who needed his help. Fate works in mysterious ways.

Overcoming Shyness

I was extremely shy around people I didn't know during my early years. Looking back there was one occasion that stands out more than others. My family and I were attending a gathering at a house across town where my siblings and I didn't know any of the other kids. I was amazed when my older brother Ted walked up to several teenagers his age and started to have a conversation by asking if they knew one of his friends who had recently moved to their area. Shortly thereafter, the conversation turned to discussing high school sports and then the upcoming season for the Detroit Lions football team. I was in awe of Ted's courage and knew at that point I wanted to be like Ted who was so outgoing in a crowd of strangers. However, it took many years before I developed such confidence.

Joining the Boy Scouts was one of the factors that helped me to overcome my shyness. To earn each merit badge, I had to phone a merit badge counselor and schedule an appointment. In many of these cases, the counselor was an adult whom I had never met and I was terrified of having to call, let alone meet with this person and present my project. These were extremely challenging experiences for me although over time, with each merit badge I earned, it became a little easier to call and meet with the next counselor.

Thus, with the help of Boy Scouts, I overcame my shyness when speaking to adults whom I didn't know.

On the other hand, my greatest fear was around girls, especially older teenage girls. Luckily, I had a break-through experience when I was in eighth grade. It happened when I was at a friend's house who had several attractive sisters. I was sitting at their family's dining room table with both my friend and his mother when his older sister walked into the room and sat down beside me. She was three years older and loved to tease me just to see me blush. On this particular day she casually draped her arm over my shoulders and with a big grin on her face said, "Don't you think it's time we become a couple?" She had performed this scene many times before and was just waiting for my face to turn bright red with embarrassment. I don't know where I summoned the courage that day, but I turned to face her and suddenly kissed her! Her face instantly turned bright red and she promptly stood up and left the room. The best part about this incident was how her mother laughed so hard that tears streamed down her face.

For some reason my friend's sister never asked me to be her boyfriend again. That incident was a turning point for me overcoming shyness and I owe my friend's sister a debt of gratitude for helping me become more confident around girls.

Winter Fun

Growing up in Michigan during the winter months could be challenging, especially when you had to walk to school in a foot of snow day-after-day. Yet Old Man Winter was forgiven when the weekend arrived and you could walk to nearby Piper Park to go sledding or to one of the numerous frozen ponds and go ice skating.

The favorite pond for skating was in Irving Park where a small island lay in the middle of the lagoon. That island made the pond a perfect oval race track. Also, the park had a heated room which allowed skaters to warm up after enduring the blistering, cold weather.

While I have many wonderful memories from Irving Park my fondest skating memory was at a remote lake north of town. I was in seventh grade when my friend Joe invited me to go ice skating with his family. As we set our skates in the back of his family's station wagon, I noticed Joe also tossed in a fully-loaded backpack. "What's in the pack?", I asked. He just grinned and said, "You'll see." The weather during the previous day had been warm enough to melt the snow on top of the frozen lake leaving a thin layer of water. Overnight the temperature dropped below freezing which turned the water into a smooth sheet of ice. As we stepped onto the frozen lake a strong gust of wind blew against our backs. That's when Joe opened his backpack, pulled out a canvas, paint tarp and handed me two corners of it. With Joe holding the other two corners, we lifted the tarp and the wind immediately inflated it creating a sail that sent us streaking across the lake far faster than either of us could have skated. When we reached the far side of the lake, Joe and I collapsed the tarp, stuffed it back into his backpack and skated back across the lake to our starting point. We ended up traversing the lake numerous times that day by first sailing across it and then skating back.

Joe always had the cleverest ideas when it came to having fun.

If it's Not Yours, Leave it Alone

A week after my first ice-sailing experience with Joe, I met him outside on a freezing night. It was so cold that I could hear the snow crunch under my feet as I walked. Joe had mentioned earlier in the day that he saw something cool and he wanted to show it to me. As I walked up to him, I said, "I hope whatever you are going to show me is worth walking in this freezing weather tonight." He nodded his head and said, "It is." We had just started walking when we heard his sister Carolyn call to us, "Hey, where are you two going?"

Me: "To see something cool. Do you want to come along?"

Carolyn: "Heck yes I want to see something cool! What is it?"

Joe: "You'll see when we get there."

We walked over to Capital Avenue and turned down an alley which I had never traveled. It sloped down a hill and about halfway into the alley we approached two garages that had a six-foot gap between them. A tall, solid-wood fence blocked the view of what lay between the two garages. As we passed the second garage, I saw what Joe wanted me to see. It was a trampoline which sat on top of four posts. There was no fence across the backyard which made the trampoline easily accessible to anyone walking down the alley. Also, the house was totally dark; it appeared no one was home.

Joe: “Pretty cool, huh?”

Me: “Yeah!”

Joe: “I’m going to jump on it for just a minute.”

Joe sat on the edge of the trampoline and started to remove his shoes.

Me: “What the heck are you doing?”

Joe: “I’m taking my shoes off.”

Me: “Why?”

Joe: “I don’t want to damage the trampoline. We always take our shoes off when we jump on the trampoline at school.”

Me: “But it’s below freezing out here!”

Joe: “Take it easy, I’m just going to take a couple of jumps and then we can head home.”

Joe stood up on the trampoline and jumped for a minute and then sat down on the edge of the trampoline. He looked at me and said, “Do you want to try it?”

I hesitated while my eyes searched each window on the back of the house for any sign of life. Upon seeing none, I replied, “Sure!”

Unlike Joe, I kept my shoes on my feet. But before I could jump, I heard a car coming down the street. The car was a good distance up the road, yet we could clearly hear it coming our way because of the roar emanating from its tailpipe. It sounded like it was missing its muffler. All three of us locked eyes on the front of the driveway which provided a byway for a car to pass from the street to the alley. To our horror, the car pulled into the driveway. Upon spotting us the driver lit the car's high-beams, sounded the horn and floored the accelerator. I jumped off the trampoline and dashed up the alley heading back towards our neighborhood. As I passed the second garage I veered right and ran to the front of the garage. When I heard the car pull into the alley on the far side of the other garage, I ducked behind a large pine tree that stood between the two garages. As I knelt behind the tree, I could hear the car racing down the alley and assumed the driver was chasing after both Joe and Carolyn. Then I heard Carolyn call my name. She had followed me around the two garages, but lost me when I ducked behind the tree. I called to her, "Over here. I'm behind this tree." As she slipped behind the tree to hide with me, I tracked the route which the car was traveling by listening to the roar from its tail pipe. The car had turned at the end of the alley, traveled around the block and was now racing back up the street to the front of the house.

Carolyn and I were well hidden behind the large pine tree, but I was concerned that if the trampoline owner spotted us, we'd be cornered between the two garages and the tall fence. However, I was also concerned that Carolyn might have a challenge attempting to climb over the fence while under duress. With the trampoline owner about to pull into the driveway I decided to take our chances and remain hidden behind the tree.

Joe didn't have time to put his shoes back on when the car had raced towards us so he fled down the snow-covered alley with socks on his feet and shoes in his hands. To ditch the car, Joe jumped over a fence and cut through another neighbor's yard where the car couldn't follow. After putting his shoes back on over snow-covered socks, Joe came back looking for us.

Meanwhile, the car pulled into the driveway and parked near the trampoline. While Carolyn and I lay in the snow behind the tree and peered out between its branches, the driver climbed out of the car and stepped onto his back porch. I could feel my heart pounding from adrenaline. The owner lit a cigarette and stood there smoking for what seemed like an eternity. Finally, he flicked the cigarette onto the snow and entered the house through the back door. Joe, who had crept back up the alley, quietly called to us from the other side of the fence. I answered with a whisper and then suggested to Carlyon we climb over the fence as opposed to walking out from behind the tree in case the trampoline owner was watching from one of the back windows. She agreed so I cupped my hands together and said, "Put your foot in my hands and your hands on my shoulders. When I count to three, push your foot down and I'll boost you up and over the fence." After Carolyn landed on the alley side of the fence, I quickly scaled the fence and the three of us tore back up the alley we had traveled earlier. We crossed Capital Avenue and ran toward our neighborhood. As we entered the alley behind my house, we stopped for a minute to catch our breath and that's when we began to laugh uncontrollably. When I finally stopped laughing, I said, "I'm never going back down that alley ever again!"

Carolyn: "Me neither!"

Joe laughed and agreed.

None of us ever went back to that trampoline and I learned an important lesson that day. If it's not yours, it's best to leave it alone.

The Dance

It was the start of ninth grade and a pack of us kids were walking to St. Phillip School for the first dance of the year. I didn't attend classes at St. Phillip, but that never stopped me from going to their extracurricular activities since many of my friends were students there. We were a block away from the school walking on the sidewalk when Abby tripped on an uneven joint between two slabs of concrete. She fell, tore her new nylons and scrapped her knee causing it to bleed. It wasn't bleeding badly, but between the blood and the torn nylons, it was enough to ruin her evening. We stood there in a quandary trying decided what to do. Should we go on to the dance in hopes of finding a first aid kit, or should we all turn around and walk Abby home where she could get patched up? Carolyn, who was the only other girl in the group that night spoke, "I'm working as a host at the dance tonight and I can't be late. Can you guys walk Abby home where she can get bandaged up?"

Johnny responded, "No way! Her house is over a mile away. I can see the school from here. We should continue on to school. They probably have a first aid kit in the office!"

Carolyn: "What if the office is locked and we can't get the first aid kit?"

Johnny: “She can clean the blood off her knee in the Girl’s room.”

Carolyn: “But her nylons are torn!”

Johnny: “Big deal!”

Carolyn refused to backdown, but paused for a moment to contemplate the situation and then turned to me and asked, “Can you walk Abby home?” I responded like I always did when a cute girl asked me for help. I said, “Sure!” To be honest, I most likely wouldn’t have volunteered to walk Abby home without first being asked since I didn’t know her very well. However, when Carolyn asked me directly, it was clearly the right action to take. Abby and I turned around and walked back to her house while our friends continued on to the dance.

Our walk turned out to be quite pleasant since we were away from the others; it gave us a chance to get to know each other better. Abby’s mother washed Abby’s scraped knee, bandaged it and gave her another pair of nylons. She then drove us to the dance where the evening continued without any other unplanned interruptions.

This incident was my first experience seeing one of us take charge of a bad situation and it provided me with a valuable lesson about how a bad scene can turn out fine when someone provides clear directions like Carolyn did that night.

Karma – Part 1

I made a boomerang in junior high by tracing a paper pattern onto a ⅜ inch sheet of marine plywood. Next, I used a jigsaw to cut the shape. With a woodworking file I rounded the top-front edge of the boomerang to make it resemble the top-front edge of an airplane wing. Finally, I filed down the rear-top edge so it would mimic the rear-top edge of a wing. This shaping provided the boomerang with the proper aerodynamics that allowed it to fly in a U-shaped path.

I gave the boomerang to my dad for his birthday and we periodically spent weekends at the park throwing it. Dad mastered the art of making the boomerang return and land right in front of his feet. This was a skill I never achieved, but one which I enjoyed practicing. Occasionally during these outings Dad would say, "That boomerang is just like karma. What goes around comes around." The following is a series of events which helped solidify both his and my belief in karma.

Dad was a member of the local Pipe Fitters/Plumbers Union and he spent his career working on construction sites. Since he typically hauled dirty tools and supplies from one construction job to another, he didn't see any sense in owning a nice new car.

Consequently, he owned undependable, used cars for most of his life. One evening, when Dad was driving home from work on the I-94 freeway, his car ran out of gas due to a broken gas gauge. After steering the car to the side of the freeway, he sat contemplating his predicament when a pickup truck pulled up next to him and the driver offered assistance. Dad accepted the offer and the stranger provided a ride to a nearby gas station. Dad purchased a new gas can filled with gasoline and the man gave him a ride back to his car. Dad offered to pay the stranger for his help, but he refused.

Over a year later, Dad was driving on I-94 again when he saw a guy wearing a baseball cap and sunglasses carrying a gas can. He was walking away from a pickup truck. Dad had never picked up hitchhikers before, but this time his heart told him to pull over. When the stranger walked up to his car, Dad offered the man a ride to the local gas station. The stranger accepted the offer and climbed into the car. Dad then realized the stranger was the same person who had given him a ride just over a year earlier. They both laughed and thought it was a strange coincidence. Dad gave the quasi stranger/friend a ride to the gas station and then took him back to his truck. The stranger thanked Dad for his help and the two parted ways, never to see each other again.

These two incidents helped cement both Dad's and my belief in karma, "What goes around comes around."

Journey to a Championship

I loved to play sports when I was growing up. There was just one problem; I was terrible at all of them. I was small for my age which was a major disadvantage when competing against bigger kids in sports like football, basketball and hockey. I also competed in high jumping in 5th and 6th grade, which was kind of funny considering my short stature. Fortunately, when I went to junior high school, I discovered wrestling. It allowed me to compete against boys who were my own size and I fell in love with the sport, such that I wrestled competitively for the next eight years and then coached a high school wrestling team for three more years.

The skills required to be a successful wrestler are similar to those needed for most other individual sports: strength, speed, agility, endurance and strategy play major roles in winning. Strategy, however, plays an even more important role in wrestling than in many other sports because of the numerous combinations of moves that can be executed like takedowns, reversals, escapes, pinning combinations, counter moves and riding styles[1].

My three seasons of wrestling in junior high school were uneventful. It was a limited program with only four schools

[1] See *Appendix* for definitions of wrestling terms.

competing so I looked forward to wrestling in high school. During my sophomore wrestling season, I was undefeated on the junior varsity team and although my varsity record was mediocre, I became adept at riding my opponents. They rarely escaped or reversed me when I was on top. Most wrestlers typically ride their opponents by holding them down using primarily their arms and hands, but I became skilled at also using my legs. This technique gave me the equivalent of four arms to wrap around my opponent in various configurations; thus, making it more challenging for my opponent to escape.

When my sophomore wrestling season ended, many of the other wrestlers went out for other sports while I decided to specialize by focusing exclusively on wrestling for the remainder of my high school years. In the spring and summer months I lifted weights with the football team and after each session I wrestled with the other wrestlers who were also weight training. In addition, I competed in freestyle wrestling tournaments during the off-season months.

All of the extra practice, conditioning and wrestling in freestyle tournaments during the off season paid off starting my junior year with wins instead of losses on the varsity squad. That year I often stayed after practice and wrestled with our head coach. He started each match by announcing, "Here we are in the state championship match between Bill Evans and Tim Kellogg." These extra matches with Coach helped me to hone my skills further.

Toward the end of the season Coach suggested I drop from the 112-pound weight class down to the 105-pound class to improve my chances in the season's final tournaments. This was not an easy decision since I was already cutting a considerable amount of weight just to make the 112-pound class. However, I did appreciate Coach's approach by making it a suggestion rather than a directive, so I cut the extra weight. The move to the 105-pound class paid off with some big wins at both the district and regional tournaments and qualified me for the state championship tournament.

I won my first two matches at the state tournament placing me in the semifinals where my opponent was a wrestler named Mick. Mick was a senior and had wrestled in the state championship the previous year. In the first 30 seconds of our match, I discovered he was no slouch when it came to wrestling. The referee had just blown his whistle to start the match when Mick grabbed my neck with his right hand and jerked my head toward my right knee. This action trapped my right foot such that I couldn't move it out of the way before Mick's left hand swooped down, seized my right ankle and yanked it out from under me. I fell flat on my rear, but managed to flip over to my base before he landed on top of me. Mick had executed a textbook example of an ankle-pick takedown and was leading 2 to 0. He then made his first of two strategic mistakes. He used a tight-waist riding style to hold me down. I immediately executed a switch maneuver and reversed Mick gaining control and earning two points, thereby tying the score at

2 to 2. While riding Mick on his right side I placed all my weight on his back as I threaded my right leg between his legs and wrapped it around his right leg while stretching my torso across his back and hooking his left arm with my right arm. I attempted to pull Mick over onto his back in what is called a guillotine pinning combination. Unfortunately, Mick was strong enough to prevent me from turning him, but I did manage to ride him through the remainder of the period.

At the end of the first period, the referee pulled a coin out of his pocket, pointed at Mick and tossed the coin in the air. Before the coin hit the mat, Mick called heads. The coin landed with its heads side up giving Mick the choice to either be on top or bottom in what is referred to as, "referee's position[2]." Mick signaled the thumbs-up gesture. The ref pointed at me and then down at the center of the mat. I knelt down on my hands and knees and Mick took the top position.

When the ref blew the whistle, I attempted to stand up, but Mick knocked me back down onto the mat. He then made his second strategic mistake when he attempted to ride me again using the same tight-waist riding style he had used in the first period. I immediately executed another switch and reversed him to lead the match 4 to 2. I used my legs again to ride Mick for the remainder of the second period and all of the third period allowing me to win the match 4 to 2. One might wonder, "What were Mick's strategic

---

[2] See *Appendix-Referee's Position*.

mistakes?" In the first 30 seconds of the match, Mick proved he was far superior to me at executing takedowns. Therefore, if instead of trying to ride me in both the first and second periods when he was on top, Mick could have let me escape allowing me to earn a single point; he most likely would have taken me down again earning another two points for the takedown. Mick could have repeated this sequence of moves earning two points for each takedown while I would have only scored a single point for each escape. Mick would have built up a wide point spread. Lucky for me, he chose to wrestle where my strengths resided, namely down on the mat as opposed to on our feet. That provided me the edge I needed to win the match.

My final match for the championship was against a wrestler named Henry. Henry was a far better wrestler than I. He was a senior; I was a junior. He had only lost twice during the season; I had lost four times. Yet I did have one advantage; I had Bill Evans as my coach and mentally I had been in the state wrestling championship dozens of times during our after-practice matches each night. You might say my mind had become conditioned to the idea of wrestling in the state finals. Thanks to Coach, I was completely calm stepping onto the mat for the state championship match.

In the first period, Henry easily countered my single-leg takedown attempt and scored two points. Next, he gained two points for a near fall. In the second period, Henry continued to dominate the match. He rode me throughout most of the period until the very end when I escaped and earned a single point, making the score 4 to 1 his favor.

In the third period I rode Henry for a minute and a half using my legs. Unfortunately, I was unable to turn him onto his back. At that point there was only 30 seconds remaining in the match and I asked myself, "How am I going to win?" I had to execute an unconventional pinning combination which Henry wouldn't expect. My only move in this category was a unique approach to the over-the-top cradle. Up till this match I had always executed a cradle like other wrestlers while riding my opponent by holding his far ankle with one hand and his near arm with the other. Fortuitously, a year earlier I had seen a unique approach to the cradle at a tournament by another wrestler. He had executed a cradle while riding his opponent with his legs. I had been using this unique approach in my practice matches after school, but I had never executed it in an official match. Now with only thirty seconds remaining I locked up an over-the-top cradle on Henry while riding him with my legs. He must have been unfamiliar with this setup to a cradle because I managed to pull him onto his back and earn two points for a near fall before he kicked out of the cradle. I now trailed Henry by one point.

I glanced over at Coach and noticed he was heading towards the scoring table to contest the referee's call. He obviously thought I should have received three points for the near fall[3] as opposed to only two. At that point, I heard our assistant coach shouting, "Do it again, Tim! Do it again! Do it again!"

Now with less than ten seconds remaining in the match I used my right forearm to cross-face Henry along the right side of his jaw and drive his head down to his left knee while threading my left arm behind his left knee, thereby allowing me to reach up and lock my hands together. As I pulled Henry onto his back again using another over-the-top cradle, I could see the match clock hanging above us and counting down the remaining seconds: 5…4…3…2…1. When the clock buzzed, I wasn't sure if I had held Henry on his back long enough to earn the additional near-fall points, but then the referee pointed his left hand at me, raised his right hand with two fingers showing and said, "Two points for near fall." I had won the state championship 5 to 4 with no time remaining on the clock!

I never dreamed of winning the state championship. My grandest goal was simply to place in the state tournament during my senior year, yet here I had won the state title my junior year. I attribute my win to the following factors. First, Coach Evans' rigorous training program which prepared me physically, such that I had enough stamina to wrestle competitively in the last 30 seconds of the match when I was behind by three points. Second, my

[3] The number of points assigned to a near fall during my era of wrestling differs from today's scoring.

teammates' commitment that forced me to wrestle my absolute best in every practice. Not only had they been excellent sparring partners during the regular wrestling season, they were also ready and willing to wrestle in the off-season at any time. This included on the mats, on our front lawns, in the sand at the beach, in our living rooms (when our parents weren't home) or any place that was semi-flat without too many obstacles that could get broken. I am in debt to both Coach and my teammates because their commitment made me into a champion.

Winning the state championship was far beyond anything I had ever dreamed. What was the lesson I learned? The harder I worked, the luckier I became.

People You Meet While Hitchhiking

Because I was involved with wrestling year-round, I never held a steady job while I was in high school. Consequently, I didn't have money to buy a car so I would hitchhike to travel around my home town. It wasn't until Labor Day weekend of my senior year when I dared to hitchhike on the freeway. My friend Troy and I had been discussing different ideas to make the coming weekend a memorable time. We decided to spend the weekend at Lake Michigan. Neither of us had a car and the lake was 90 miles away; therefore, hitchhiking was our only option.

It was raining on the morning we left town and within the first hour both Troy and I were drenched. At one point a semitruck passed us and created such a wave of water and wind that it blew our ponchos off and we had to run into a farmer's field to retrieve them. Luckily, we were able to hitch our rides fairly quickly. This most likely was due to the bad weather and our drivers feeling sorry for us standing in the pouring rain.

Of all the rides we received that day my most memorable was with a young, African American man who picked us up on the west side of Kalamazoo. He was wearing a fedora and as we climbed into his car, we thanked him for the ride. Without saying a word, he nodded his head, shifted the car into drive, stepped on the accelerator and proceeded to race down the freeway at 90 mph. I have to admit I breathed a sigh of relief when he took an exit ramp just a few miles down the road and dropped us off. As we climbed out of his car, we thanked him again for the ride. He nodded his head as he had done previously and without saying a word he stepped on the accelerator and flew down the exit ramp. You definitely meet some interesting people when you hitchhike. Some drivers pick you up because they are bored and they want to talk with you while other drivers just want to help by giving you a ride.

A couple of hours later we arrived at Lake Michigan. The sun came out from behind the clouds and dried both us and our gear. We spent the next two days swimming in the lake, sunning ourselves on the beach during the day and sleeping on the sand dunes at night. On Labor Day afternoon we headed back home.

Our second ride was with Bob, who was heading to a sales call in our home town. Bob had hitched a lot of rides in his younger days and had plenty advice to bestow upon Troy and me. For example, always have a sign that informs a potential ride where you are heading. If a driver feels like talking to someone during a long ride, he doesn't want to pick up a hitchhiker who is going to be dropped off only a few miles down the road. Secondly, include an interesting tagline on your sign that informs a potential driver that you are a good conversationalist or you have a sense of humor. For example, if you are heading to Chicago, your sign might say, "Chicago, I tell great stories."

This hitchhiking trip to Lake Michigan and Bob's advice gave me the courage to undertake my most audacious and foolish endeavor ever in the not-too-distant future[4].

[4] See *More People You Meet While Hitchhiking*.

Journey to a Second Championship

After winning the state championship during my junior year in high school, I felt enormous pressure to repeat this feat during my senior year. I was often asked by friends, relatives and sometimes total stranger: "Are you going to win state this coming year?" My dilemma was how to answer this question. If I answered honestly with, "I have no idea.", I was perceived as lacking confidence. On the other hand, if I said, "Absolutely!", I was perceived as being cocky. I ended up replying, "Come see."

It was likely apparent by the description of my matches during the previous year how lucky I was to win the championship. It may also have been noted that the weakest aspect of my wrestling style was my takedown ability. To address this deficiency, I wrestled in as many freestyle tournaments as possible during the off-season between my junior and senior year. These tournaments focused primarily on takedowns. They allowed me to perfect the fireman-carry, single-leg and duck-under takedowns which would play a major role in my success during the coming season. Besides participating in freestyle tournaments, I lifted weights with our football team and wrestled with my teammates after each weight-lifting session. To focus my mind, I made a poster that read *Take State* and tacked it to my bedroom wall. Thereafter, every morning when I woke up, the first thing I saw was that poster. It was a constant reminder of my number one purpose in life during the coming year.

The first part of my senior wrestling season went well. I built up 17 consecutive wins with no losses. Sadly, this streak came to a crashing halt eight weeks prior to the state championship when on a Saturday afternoon I lost two matches and tied the third. It was not a good day for me to say the least. Of the three opponents I wrestled that day, only one was a major concern. His name was Stuart and he was not only extremely strong, but he had also honed his moves to be exceptionally fast. The final score of our match was 11 to 8. The fact that Stuart scored eleven points against me was not a good omen.

Nonetheless, this loss was to my advantage down the road because I now knew most of his favorite moves. I spent many subsequent evenings replaying that match like a video tape in my mind. With each move I envisioned Stuart executing, I would visualize how I would counter it. Thus, when I stepped onto the mat at the state championship two months later to wrestle Stuart for the state title, he had wrestled me just once. I, on the other hand, had wrestled him once in real life, but dozens of times in my mind.

Within the first few seconds of the state championship match, I attempted to take Stuart down with a fireman-carry. Unfortunately, as I reached with my right hand to grab his left bicep, Stuart shot a single-leg takedown under my arm and swept my leg out from under me, scoring two points. I immediately stood up and executed a standing switch. It had always given me a reversal for two points against other wrestlers, but it didn't work that way with Stuart. He was too strong for me to complete the switch. I managed only to escape, earning just one point.

At the end of the first period, I was behind 2 to 1. Stuart won the coin toss and chose the top position to start the second period. Again, I stood up and managed to escape, gaining another point and evening the score 2 to 2. I now shot a fireman-carry takedown scoring two more points making the score 4 to 2 in my favor.

During our first match, Stuart easily reversed me when I used a traditional leg-riding style. This time I rode him using the figure-four style which was rarely used. It allowed me to ride him throughout the remainder of the second period and all of the third period. It was during the third period when I turned Stuart onto his back using a half-nelson pinning combination that I scored an additional two points for a near fall. Our final match score was 6 to 2 my favor which gave me my second state title.

As I mentioned in *Fearless*, when something doesn't go your way, it might be in your best interest. If I hadn't wrestled Stuart earlier in the season, I wouldn't have learned his favorite moves and I wouldn't have been as prepared to wrestle him in the state finals. Wrestling Stuart early in the season was truly a blessing even though at the time when I lost to him, I thought it was the worst day of my life.

The best way to sum up the lesson I learned from this experience is a quote from Nelson Mandela:

"I never lose. I either win or I learn."

In the Wrong Place at the Wrong Time

After winning my second state championship, Coach Evans sent my wrestling resume to several college coaches. Within weeks I received calls from those coaches, one of whom was the head coach at Oklahoma University (OU). I was invited to visit Norman, Oklahoma on an all-expense-paid trip to see the campus and to meet some of their wrestlers. I was very impressed with what I saw and within a couple of weeks I signed a Letter of Intent to attend OU. Five months later I was living in Norman and going to classes.

I had only been on the OU campus for a week when my new friend Jim and I went to a local tavern one evening. As we entered the tavern, Jim saw two girls he knew from high school. They invited us to join them. After talking for about thirty minutes, the girls suggested all four of us go to their dorm room for a game of cards. Jim and I accepted the offer and walked with them. We entered the lobby and took an elevator up to their room. After playing cards for about an hour I bid them goodnight. I had an 8:00 am class the next morning, but Jim didn't have a class until 10:00 am so he stayed behind. I took the elevator down to the first floor and when I stepped out of the elevator, I heard someone shout, "What do you think you're doing?" I looked around the lobby to see who was shouting and only saw a young security guard, who looked to be my age. I responded, "I'm just leaving."

Guard: "No you're not!"

Me: "I don't understand. What's the problem?"

The guard pointed to the elevator and roared, "Those girls' rooms are off-limits after 9:00 pm!"

I scanned the wall and spotted the sign: "Visiting Hours End at 9:00 pm." I also noticed the wall clock read 9:35 pm. I had clearly erred by not reading the signage when first entering the lobby. In an attempt to plead with the guard, I turned the palms of my hands face up and said, "Hey buddy, this is the first time I've been in this dorm and I didn't see the sign. It won't happen again. Can you just let me go this time?"

Guard: "No way, boy! You're in big trouble!"

The guard didn't have a gun on his utility belt so I bolted for the exit door. I hit the door running full speed with the guard right behind me and as I ran across the lawn, I could hear not only his footsteps pounding the ground behind me, but his panting breath like a bull charging a red cape. I also heard chains jangling which I assumed were the handcuffs he pulled from his utility belt. At that moment I became cognizant of a seven-foot-tall hedge directly in front of me which was about 40 yards wide. Now I'm not a fast runner, but with adrenalin pumping through every muscle in my body, I was running faster than I had ever run in my entire life. Also, I don't normally think fast. Oh, I can come up with a solution for most problems, but it takes a while, like maybe a day or two. Unfortunately, I only had a few seconds before my escape route dead-ended into that huge hedge. I thought about running around it. But with the guard right behind me, I feared any veering would slow me down to the point where the guard could tackle me. It was at this point I noticed a few scattered lights shining through the hedge from the other side. I made a quick assumption that those scattered lights represented where the hedge was the least dense.

It's amazing how fast our brains work when we are under pressure. As I approached the hedge, a similar scenario from six years earlier flashed through my mind. It was a late summer evening and I was playing the game ditch'em with several of my neighborhood friends. We had two teams; one team scattered and hid throughout the neighborhood while the other team tried to find and tag each of the other team's members. Once everyone was tagged, it was the other team's turn to hide. I was hiding in a neighbor's backyard when one of my friends from the other team spotted me. There was a thick hedge along one side of the yard so I decided to run to the hedge and duck through it. My friend was quite a bit bigger than me and I figured he'd get tangled up trying to follow me through the thick hedge. What I didn't know was that on the opposite side of the hedge stood a wire fence. I hit the fence running full speed and upon impact, the force ricocheted me backwards such that I landed flat on my back. I was totally dazed from ramming into that fence and all I remember is seeing my friend laughing hysterically as he casually walked over, kicked my foot and said, "Gotcha!"

Here I was six years later in a similar scenario. I had no idea whether a fence or some other obstacle lay on the opposite side of the tall hedge. But the last thing I needed was to be arrested and have to call my wrestling coach to bail me out of jail. Therefore, when I was two steps before hitting the hedge at full speed, I gambled by pulling my knees up to my chest, tucking my face down into my knees and wrapping my arms around my head. I shot through the hedge like a cannon ball. Luckily, there was no fence or any other obstacle on the far side. As my feet touched the ground, I heard the most awful cry from the guard, "Ahhhhhhhh!" He must have slammed into the hedge while running upright. Without looking back, I sprinted away zigzagging between buildings in case the guard was still chasing me. When I finally stopped and looked back, it was all clear. The guard was probably still untangling himself from the hedge. I ran up the back stairs of the dorm to my room and luckily no one came looking for me. I was safe! I called the girl's room and asked them to tell Jim to take the fire escape stairs and not the elevator; thus, allowing him to dodge the security guard.

I learned many lessons that night, but my most important take-away was to be cognizant of my surroundings especially when in a new environment. In other words, read the signage!

More People You Meet While Hitchhiking

A couple of days before Christmas I rode home from OU with Ken, who was also from Michigan. We only stayed a few days before returning to Norman for five days of wrestling practices. Then the varsity team (including Ken) left for a west-coast wrestling tour. The rest of the team was free to go home for another week of vacation before classes resumed. The only problem was that my home was over 600 miles away in Michigan and the OU campus was like a ghost town. At that point I made the boldest and most foolish decision of my life when I decided to hitchhike home.

My friend Will gave me a ride to his home in Tulsa, putting me 100 miles closer to my home. That night, following Bob's advice from my prior hitchhiking trip to Lake Michigan[5], I created a cardboard sign for the upcoming trek. The top of the sign read, "Check Your Brakes." The bottom portion of the sign consisted of three layers of cardboard where the top two layers were stapled on top of the bottom section. Each layer listed the next major city on my journey. The topmost layer said, "St. Louis"; next was

[5] See *People You Meet While Hitchhiking.*

"Chicago" and the bottom layer said, "Battle Creek", my hometown.

Will dropped me off at the I-44 onramp in Tulsa the following morning. The temperature sign on the bank building read 10° Fahrenheit and I had a minimum ten-hour journey ahead. I proudly held up my newly designed sign and waited for the first ride. I stood shivering with a strong north wind blowing in my face when a brown van pulled up. The young driver greeted me and introduced himself as Rich. Rich was on his way back to dental school in St. Louis which would place me 300 miles closer to home. I scored big on this first ride!

As we cruised north, we talked while listening to the radio. After about thirty minutes, Rich asked, "Have you ever run into any trouble while hitchhiking?" I casually said, "Nah, nothing I couldn't handle." Rich replied, "That's good." and then he smiled while saying, "Just make sure there's a door handle on the inside of the door!" I laughed and said, "Will do!" and then quickly glanced down to confirm there was a door handle. Wow! It had never occurred to me to check if there was a door handle on the inside of a stranger's car door. Thank goodness the door handle was there! I made a note to myself: "Always check for a door handle when entering a stranger's car. Also, hold on to the handle (not the armrest) when closing the door to confirm the handle is attached."

I have to say that during my years of hitchhiking, 99% of the people I met were wonderful. The remaining 1% were downright scary.

It was almost 2:00 pm when we reached St. Louis where Rich dropped me off. I thanked him for the ride and as I got out of his van, I removed the piece of cardboard from my sign which read "St. Louis" and asked Rich to properly dispose of it. The bottom portion of the sign now read, "Chicago." It took several short rides to traverse the outer beltway of St. Louis before I was heading north on I-55 to Chicago.

As the day progressed, I became concerned. The window of opportunity for catching rides was shrinking. I needed to reach Chicago before nightfall, or I could become stranded at a dimly lit ramp where drivers would be less likely to pick up a hitchhiker. What complicated this goal was that several drivers offered to buy me lunch or dinner. I politely declined, citing my need to travel as much distance as possible while there was still daylight. Amazingly, many of these drivers generously gave me money to help me buy a meal for when I had time to stop and eat.

The sun had been down for over an hour when I reached Chicago, but the highway ramps were well lit. A small MG sports car picked me up. The driver's name was Stacy and she had long, blonde, curly hair. I was thankful for the ride, but I was also astonished that she picked me up while driving alone at night. For the next 30 minutes we chatted about the people I met while hitchhiking.

Then Stacy pulled off the freeway at her exit. I thanked her for the ride and asked if she could do me a favor.

She hesitated before saying, "Maybe."

Me: "Please! Never pick up another hitchhiker while driving alone! There are just too many unpredictable people out here."

Stacy laughed and said, "Okay."

As I left Stacy's car, I noticed a soldier in uniform standing a few yards up the ramp.

I spoke, "Mind if I hitch with you?"

Soldier: "No problem. I'm John."

Me: "Thanks! I'm Tim."

By the virtue of good luck, we quickly hitched a ride with two, young, Latino guys who were driving an Oldsmobile 442 muscle car heading to Benton Harbor, Michigan. Our ride was making great time, but after an hour John spoke up and said he needed to get off at the next exit. When we dropped John off, it left me alone with my two new friends who were consuming beers fairly rapidly. All of a sudden, the car pulled off the road in the middle of nowhere and I began to panic. Normally I wasn't afraid of any one driver, but if these two guys wanted trouble, it was going to be a challenge. Thankfully, the driver turned around and said, "Hey man, we gotta piss. Do you gotta piss?"

Me: “No man, I’m fine.”

Driver: “Okay, we’ll be right back.”

After a few minutes we were back on the road and an hour later my friends reached their exit at Benton Harbor, Michigan where they dropped me off near the onramp. I stood there for an hour as the temperature continued to drop. Finally, I decided it was too dark and too late for anyone to consider picking up a hitchhiker so I walked to a nearby motel and with cash in hand asked the clerk if there were any rooms available.

He responded: “Are you 21-years old or older?”

Me: “No.”

Clerk: “Sorry, our hotel rules require you to be at least 21 to rent a room.”

I turned and walked away not saying a word. There was no point in debating the issue. The clerk was just doing his job. With the temperature approaching 0° Fahrenheit I decided it was time to phone my parents. I had been traveling for 14 hours and was less than two hours away from home so using a pay phone I called. When my mom answered, I told her my location and she replied, “We’re on our way.” I can’t tell you how happy I was to see my dad’s car pull into the motel parking lot. I spent the next week at home and when it was time for me to return back to Norman, my parents purchased an airplane ticket for me.

I have to say my hitchhiking trip from Oklahoma to Michigan in the middle of winter was my most foolish endeavor ever! In the following years there were several times where I couldn't catch a ride for hours when hitchhiking. I was very fortunate to have received the numerous rides in such a short amount of time from so many generous drivers during that hike from Oklahoma to Michigan. Maybe it was my custom-made sign that caused the drivers to stop and pick me up, or maybe it was divine intervention. Either way, I realize now that I was both very lucky and over confident.

If anyone were to ask me today, "Do you recommend hitchhiking?", I'd say, "Absolutely not!" It just doesn't seem to be as safe now as it did back then, or maybe I'm just wiser. Although, if you ever must hitchhike, before you close the car door, make sure there's an inside-door handle and it's intact!

Greek Mythology

It was the last week of spring term and I was in the cafeteria having lunch when Gus and Mike sat down at the table. We had some classes together and had become good friends. Gus had recently injured his knee and had been waiting for the last few weeks to have the surgery scheduled to repair it.

Me: “How’s it going guys?”

Gus: “Not well.”

Me: “What’s up?”

Gus: “I was just notified that my surgery is scheduled for tomorrow morning. Apparently, another surgery was canceled and they want me to have my knee repaired tomorrow.”

Me: “Isn’t that good news? You been waiting for weeks to have this surgery.”

Gus: “Yes, but the final exam for my Greek Mythology class is also scheduled for tomorrow morning and I’ve been studying for it all week.”

Me: “I’m sorry to hear that, Gus.”

Mike then looked at me with a devilish smile and said, "Maybe you can help him."

Me: "What do you mean?"

Mike: "You can take his test for him."

I laughed and replied, "Guys, I don't know anything about Greek Mythology!"

Mike: "That's not a problem."

Me: "Really! How so?"

Mike: "This class has over 90 students and it is held in a huge auditorium."

Me: "So?"

Mike: "I'm also in the class. All you have to do is follow me into the class and sit directly behind me. The test consists of all multiple-choice questions. Every couple of minutes I'll lift my exam up as if I'm reading it carefully so you can see my answers and write them down on Gus' test."

A side note: I had never cheated on a test, nor had I helped another student cheat. However, Gus had given me numerous rides during the past school year. Therefore, I owed him a favor.

Me: "Gus, are you sure you want me to take this test?"

Gus: “I would greatly appreciate it!”

Me: “Okay, but if this plan fails, I can’t be held responsible for your test results.”

Gus: “No problem Tim. I’m sure it will be fine.”

I was extremely nervous the next day as I walked with Mike to the history hall and sat directly behind him in an aisle seat. As the tests were being handed out, I noticed several teacher aides walking up and down the aisle obviously assigned to watch for unethical behavior. Fortunately, everything seemed to be going as planned. Every couple of minutes Mike lifted his test up close to his face as if he was reading it carefully and I marked his answers on Gus’ test. All of a sudden one of the teacher aides, who was standing in my row across the room, started walking briskly toward me with a stern look on her face. It was obvious she had seen me looking at Mike’s test and was coming to confiscate my test. To my surprise, as she crossed the aisle next to me, she took a sidestep, reached down underneath Mike’s desk and yanked several sheets of paper from his hand. Unbeknown to me, Mike had been “referencing” a set of crib notes in his lap. The aide pointed to the exit door and Mike slowly walked out the exit, head hanging down.

I was now in a predicament; I had only completed the answers to the first half of the test, and Mike was no longer available to help. With no other option I used the process of elimination to answer the remaining multiple-choice questions. Luckily, I had the advantage of knowing the answers to the first half of the test which provided some insight to the remaining questions. Thirty minutes later, I submitted Gus' test. The next day I was in the cafeteria when Mike walked in and sat down. I said, "I'm really sorry about your final exam, Mike."

Mike: "No problem. It was my fault. But guess what?"

Me: "I give up."

Mike: "They posted the test results and you scored 71% on Gus' test! He passed!"

Me: "Wow! That's great news! Have you told Gus?"

Mike: "Yes and he's very happy. Also, his surgery went well."

Me: "Thank goodness!"

I learned an important lesson from this experience. Even though I justified my unethical action because I was helping a friend in need, I was clearly wrong. I made a note to myself that if this type of situation ever occurred in the future, I would suggest my friend ask his professor to take the test at another time. I later found that most professors are fairly flexible concerning these types of requests, especially when you have a good excuse.

Playing One's Only Ace

Even though I haven't lived in my hometown for decades I still read the obituaries from the newspaper website. They provide an avenue for me to stay in touch with my past as well as the opportunity to send condolences to friends who have lost loved ones. Recently I read the obituary for one of my childhood friends. The obituary was very short, but it brought back a long-forgotten memory.

It was during the summer between my freshman and sophomore year in college and I was working a construction job. Because there was no dress code, I let my hair grow long enough that it touched my shoulders. Also, I was outside all day in the sun so the color of my hair was bleached blond and not its normal color.

One evening I was walking to a friend's house when I noticed a couple of guys staring at me. After a minute they began walking toward me. When they were within 25 yards they broke into a sprint and charged. I couldn't help but notice the angry looks on their faces. I had never observed a mugging, but this scene had all the markings of one. Luckily, their hands were empty and appeared to have no weapons. I then realized I had an advantage over these would-be attackers. Instead of turning and running away, I stood my ground, waited until they were only a few yards away and then played my only ace when I calmly said, “Hi Gavin.” My words abruptly stopped Gavin and his associate dead in their tracks with their mouths’ gaping.

Me: “How’s it going?”

Gavin’s face changed from one of outrage to a large grin. “Tim! I’m doing good. Boy, I haven’t seen you in ages. I didn’t recognize you with your long, blond hair!”

Me: “Yeah, I let it grow out for the summer and the sun has bleached it.”

It had been years since I last saw Gavin who had dropped out of high school. There was a time in elementary and junior high when we were good friends and I had spent a lot of summer afternoons at his house.

Me: “So, what have you been up to?”

Gavin: “Not much. Just looking for work. Hey, would you have a few dollars you could loan me? We haven’t eaten anything since yesterday.”

Me: “Sure!” I pulled a ten-dollar bill out of my wallet (the only money I had) and gave it to him.

Gavin: “Thanks Tim! I’ll pay you back next time I see you.”

Me: "Nope. You don't have to pay me back. Consider it a payment for all the times your family fed me when I was hanging out at your house in junior high."

Gavin: "Those were some great times!

Me: "Yes they were! Hey buddy, I'm running late and need to get going. We'll have to get together soon. Why don't you give me a call when you have a chance?"

Gavin: "Will do and thanks again Tim. Take care!"

There had been a time in our lives when Gavin and I were good friends, but that was many years before this encounter and we had fallen out of touch. The interesting point to ponder is whether or not there was ill intent planned when Gavin and his buddy rushed me. If there was ill intent, I'm glad I was their target. Since I knew Gavin, I foiled their plan. Secondly, I was able to freely provide Gavin and his associate with funds to eat, relieving them from taking any unethical action they might have regretted. I later heard that Gavin was hired as a janitor and seemed to be doing okay.

Sometimes a person just needs a little help during a difficult situation, like when he hasn't eaten for the past 24 hours.

A Parent's Love

After attending Oklahoma University for a year and a half on a wrestling scholarship, my desire to wrestle competitively had passed. I had been wrestling for the past eight years and I was burned out due to the weight-cutting and stress that went along with the sport. It was the first weekend in January and I was sitting at my parent's kitchen table with my dad. Two days earlier I had called home and told my mom I was done wrestling and I was coming home. I was now preparing myself for the consequences of my decision.

Dad spoke, "When you were a senior in high school, several college coaches recruited you to wrestle for them, perhaps you could go wrestle for one of them now."

Me: "I have no desire to wrestle in college anymore. I'm done!"

Dad: "Good!"

I was stunned by his response. Here I had made the decision to walk away from a college-wrestling scholarship and he seemed happy. Of all the possible responses I had anticipated from him, "Good!" was not one of them. My attitude abruptly changed from being fearful to being indignant. I responded, "What do you mean by good?"

Dad: "Your mother and I are glad you are getting out of the sport before you get seriously injured."

Me: "How long have you felt this way?"

Dad: "A long time."

Again, I was stunned. My parents had supported me completely in my wrestling endeavors. They attended almost all of my meets; but more importantly, they tolerated my surly attitude when I was starving myself to make weight. They never said a word about having concerns with me being a wrestler. Many parents would have forbidden their son from participating in an activity that concerned them, but my parents didn't say a word about their feelings. Instead, they supported me wholeheartedly. I believe this to be one of the best examples of a parent's true love for their child.

It has been many years since I had that conversation with my dad. Both of my parents are now gone; however, the lessons I learned from them have stayed with me. I have tried to follow their example in raising my own children. I've bitten my tongue upon numerous occasions to not discourage them from following their own dreams even when I had concerns. I was very fortunate to have had parents who taught me how to be a good parent through their own actions.

Looking back at my decision to quit wrestling competitively, it was one of the most difficult decisions I ever made, but it was also one of my best decisions. It allowed me to focus on my college studies and major in mathematics. This decision opened the door to computer science and a career in high technology. It also gave me the opportunity to coach a high school wrestling team for three years while completing my bachelor's degree and thereby allowed me to repay the sport that had given me so much. And most importantly, I met Lori from my hometown whom I would eventually marry.

Life is made up of decisions we have to make. And after we've made them, all we can do is move on and be open to what life offers us next.

Who Said That?

After leaving Oklahoma and returning home, I enrolled at a local community college which is where I first met Lori. I must not have made much of an impression on her because when I met her a second time, she didn't remember meeting me previously. Fortunately, we began seeing each other quite often at various parties around our hometown.

The following autumn two of our friends were married and both Lori and I were in their wedding. We had a wonderful time during the wedding reception and afterwards we went four-wheel riding with our friend John in his SUV. There's nothing like off-road riding in the woods at night and having the SUV's radiator hose burst. Luckily, John had a roll of duct tape which he used to temporarily patch the hose, allowing us to get back into town where we stopped at a coffee shop. It was while we were having coffee that Lori asked me, "Do you ever date girls who are taller than you?" I replied, "Of course!" and I didn't say anything more. Obviously, I missed her hint since she was slightly taller than I (was).

About a week later Lori called and asked me to go with her to see a concert starring the group Chicago. Regrettably, I had a class the night of the concert and our midterm exam was scheduled for that night. Consequently, I couldn't go to the concert unless I skipped class which would have been unwise since I had found the class to be quite challenging. Strangely though, when I responded to Lori's invitation, an eerie thing happened. It was like a spirit hijacked my voice and started speaking for me. Instead of saying, "I'm sorry Lori, I can't go with you to the concert because I have a midterm exam that night." I heard my voice say, "Sure, I would love to go with you to the concert!"

After getting off the phone and panicking for the next couple of days I decided my best option was to speak to my professor who turned out to be very sympathetic when I told him I couldn't attend class during the night of the midterm. He offered me the option to take the exam on a different night. That was a huge relief!

Lori and I had a fabulous time at the concert and we started dating regularly. Often during our weekend dates, we would go out to eat at a local pizza parlor. It was during our first pizza parlor visit when the hijacking voice returned. We just sat down and were looking over the menu when Lori enthusiastically said, "What should we order on our pizza? How about mushrooms and pepperoni?" That's when I heard my voice reply, "Sounds good!" I then asked myself, "Who in the heck said that?" I surely didn't say, "Sounds good." because I hated mushrooms! I had only eaten a mushroom once in my whole life and I gagged on it. It wasn't just the taste of mushrooms I didn't like; I could never tell the difference between the poisonous mushrooms and the edible mushrooms. Consequently, I was always paranoid that some poisonous mushrooms might accidentally be intermixed with edible ones. Yet here I'd agreed to eat mushrooms on a pizza. For the next six months whenever Lori and I went out for pizza, I found my voice being hijacked again and again. Each time I smiled and agreed to eat mushrooms on the pizza. Finally, one night before we ordered a pizza, I heard my own voice sneak out a sentence and say, "I suppose you want mushrooms on the pizza?" Lori looked up from her menu with a surprised expression on her face and said, "What? You don't like mushrooms?"

Me: "Hmm, not really."

Lori: "But you've been eating mushrooms on pizza with me for the last six months."

Me: "Yeah I know."

Lori: "Why didn't you say something?"

This is when I heard my own debonaire voice speak up and say, "I don't know."

Lori: "Wow, you must really like me if you were willing to eat mushrooms on pizza with me for the last six months. How about we order the pizza with just half of it covered with mushrooms?"

Me: "That's a great idea!"

And that's how my future wife and I negotiated our first big agreement.

The best lesson I learned from this experience is that a 50/50 split is almost always a good solution when negotiating.

How Our Perspective Changes

I grew up in a neighborhood where the typical house didn't include an attached garage like houses built today. Instead, each house had its garage located directly behind it on an alley which ran through the middle of the neighborhood block. The doors on many of these garages opened by swinging outward, like a pair of French doors. These doors were usually left open because remote garage door openers were not available at that time. I was ten years old when my friends and I realized that the cross-support boards on the inside of these doors could be used like rungs on a ladder, allowing us to climb up the doors and onto the garage roof[6], thereby giving us a nice view of the neighborhood.

One of our favorite garage roofs belonged to Mr. Miller. The rear of his garage was positioned next to another garage so we would lie on the backside of his garage roof between the two garages where we were less likely to be seen. Unfortunately, sometimes Mr. Miller would spot us and come storming out his backdoor hollering, "Get off my roof, Tim Kellogg!" My friends and I would jump across the three-foot gap between the roofs, run to the far

[6]Note that these roof climbing escapades occurred prior to the lesson I learned when jumping on a stranger's trampoline. See *If it's Not Yours, Leave it Alone*.

side of the other roof, leap to the soft lawn below and run away laughing. Luckily, we never broke any bones which I believe was Mr. Miller's primary concern.

Many years later I was walking down the alley by Mr. Miller's garage and noticed he was attempting to install a large light fixture over his garage door while standing on an old, rickety, wooden stepladder. He was holding the light fixture with one hand while trying to use a drill with his other hand to screw the base of the fixture into the garage wall. As I walked by, I called out, "Need any help?"

When Mr. Miller turned around and saw me, he replied, "I sure could! Can you climb up on the far side of this ladder and hold this light fixture while I install these screws?"

Me: "Sure!"

When I climbed up on the far side of the ladder, it started to wobble. That's when Mr. Miller said, "Maybe you should climb up on the roof and hold the light fixture from there."

Me: "Okay, but there was a time when you used to yell at me for climbing on this roof."

Mr. Miller laughed and said, "I'll make an exception for you this time, Tim."

After we finished attaching the light fixture I climbed off the roof and Mr. Miller asked, "How's college going for you?"

Me: "It's going well. I'll graduate next year."

Mr. Miller: "Isn't this your fourth year in college?"

Me: "Yep!"

Mr. Miller: "I thought college only took four years?"

Me: "Yep."

Mr. Miller: "So why is it taking you five years?"

Me: "Well, I'm majoring in mathematics and to get through college in only four years with a major in mathematics, you have to either be really smart, or you have to study an enormous number of hours. My problem is I'm neither that smart, nor am I willing to study that many hours."

Mr. Miller laughed and replied: "Well Tim, at least you're honest with yourself. Thanks for helping me install that light fixture."

Me: "No problem Mr. Miller. You take care."

I guess Mr. Miller forgave me for climbing on his garage roof all those times so many years ago. Since then, my perspective has changed. For example, if I ever catch a neighborhood kid climbing on my garage roof, I'll holler, "Get off my roof!" just like

Mr. Miller used to holler at me. But I'll have to quickly look away so my grin won't be noticed.

Coaching Wrestling

I had the good fortune to coach a high school wrestling team while attending Western Michigan University. The school was located in a small farming community about thirty miles north of my hometown. Each weekday morning, I drove to Kalamazoo to attend classes and afterwards I drove out to the high school.

I was the assistant coach during my first year of coaching; there was very little pressure in this position. Sadly, shortly after the first wrestling season ended, our head coach was injured in a motorcycle accident which forced him to retire. The next season I was hired as the head coach. I had a young team which meant I had several freshmen and sophomores in the varsity line up. The toughest aspect of being the head wrestling coach was when I sent a freshman or sophomore out to wrestle a junior or senior wrestler from another team. These older wrestlers typically had far greater strength than the younger wrestlers and often gave my wrestlers a terrible beating.

During my second year as head coach, the team improved considerably. My wrestlers had matured and we were winning more matches. When the two-week Christmas break arrived, I informed the team we would be practicing throughout most of the break. Our school was hosting its own tournament on the last Saturday of the break and I wanted my team to wrestle well for the hometown crowd. On the first day of Christmas break practice, I told the wrestlers we were going win our tournament. This statement astonished several of the senior wrestlers and made them laugh. They reminded me that our most fierce competitor, the Saxons, would be wrestling in our tournament and they had trounced us in the previous year's dual meet. I was prepared for this response. I told them:

> "This year is going to be different from last year and I'll give you four reasons why. First: The Saxons had several of their best wrestlers graduate last year so they are not as tough this year. Second: You've matured and you are physically stronger and more confident than you were last year. Third: Last year we wrestled the Saxons at their school which gave them a psychological advantage. This year we are going to be wrestling them in our own gymnasium which will give us the advantage. And finally, the fourth and most important reason we are going win our tournament is because we are going to be in better shape than any Saxon wrestler. We are going to practice throughout most of this Christmas break. If the Saxons do practice, they won't be working out nearly as often or as hard as we do. Thus, when you step onto the mat in our gym you are going to have more stamina than any Saxon wrestler. A Saxon wrestler might lead a match against us

during the first period, but in the second or third period, we will come from behind and we will win!"

For the next two weeks during our grueling practices, I continued to emphasize my four points of how we were going to win. In reality, I didn't think we had a chance, but I wanted my wrestlers to at least be competitive.

Wrestling is an individual sport where a wrestler competes solely against his or her opponent on the mat, but I firmly believe that team spirit is a contributing factor to winning. Knowing there are eleven teammates on the side rooting for you and greeting you when you come off the mat, regardless of whether you've won or lost, makes a huge difference in how you wrestle.

To help build team spirit I threw a surprise Christmas party after practice the day before Christmas Eve. The night before the party I stayed up late with my wife and several of her younger siblings making Christmas cookies and treats. It was an excellent way to end the last practice before Christmas. In addition to providing a Christmas party for the team, one day after practice we carpooled to a winter sports park where we had fun sliding down the steep toboggan runs together. These events helped build a camaraderie between the wrestlers.

When the day of the tournament arrived, my wrestlers didn't let me down. We had sophomores beating juniors and seniors from the other teams. When the final round began for first and second places in each weight class, we had five wrestlers competing while our major rival, the Saxons, had six wrestlers. The final match to determine the championship team was between our wrestler, Tony, and a Saxon wrestler named Wade. Tony's record coming into the tournament was 5 wins 6 losses. Wade's record was 11 wins 2 losses. Wade was his team's star wrestler and was highly favored to win the match. To make the situation even more interesting, Wade had to pin Tony for his team to win the tournament; otherwise, we would win the tournament. As Tony was warming up for his match, I pulled him aside. In this situation, I had heard some coaches say to their wrestlers, "Just don't get pinned." I loathed those words because they contradicted my coaching philosophy of making each wrestler into a champion. To make a wrestler into a champion, you had to make him believe he was a champion. Hence, you never say to a wrestler, "Just don't get pinned."

Me: "Tony, you're in better shape than Wade. Right?"

Tony: "Yes Coach."

Me: "So no matter what happens in the first or second period, you just keep going after him because by the third period he's going to get tired. Right?"

Tony: "Right Coach! I won't quit!"

Me: "I know you won't. Now go out there and win yourself a championship!"

Tony: "Okay Coach."

Let me tell you about Tony. He was a good kid who worked hard during practice and got along well with all the other wrestlers. I never heard him say anything negative. In fact, I never heard him say much. He was a very quiet individual. It appeared he didn't have much money because he wore tennis shoes to school year-round, even through the winter months when there was a foot of snow on the ground.

During our first, all-day Saturday tournament that season, one of the other wrestlers mentioned Tony wasn't eating. When I asked Tony why, he said, "I don't have any money." I offered to buy him lunch, but he refused, saying "I don't need charity!" I thought about Tony's situation for the next hour before realizing we had left the medical kit on the school bus. I offered to buy Tony a lunch if he fetched the kit and then return it to the bus after the tournament ended. Tony agreed, which allowed him to earn his lunch with dignity. From that point on, Tony was responsible for our medical kit during Saturday tournaments.

There was an interesting aspect concerning Tony's wrestling ability compared to how the other team members wrestled. When our team was wrestling poorly, Tony tended to wrestle poorly. However, when our team was wrestling well, Tony wrestled great! Fortunately, on the day of the tournament, our team was wrestling the best I had ever seen. Likewise, during Tony's first two matches he had wrestled exceptionally well.

Both our fans and the Saxon's fans knew the team championship was going to be decided by the match between Tony and Wade. When the referee blew the whistle to start the match, all the fans from both schools stood up and began shouting for their wrestler. Within the first 30 seconds Wade used a double-leg takedown to take Tony to the mat and put him on his back. Tony managed to get off his back without getting pinned. Wade had gained four points: two for the takedown and two for the near fall. Next Wade put Tony on his back again, gaining another two points, for another near fall. Tony managed to get off his back again, stood up and escaped, allowing him to earn one point. The first period ended with the score 6 to 1, Wade's favor.

At the start of the second period, Wade was in the down position. When the referee blew his whistle, Wade immediately stood up and escaped from Tony. It was at this point Wade made a strategic mistake. He attempted to throw Tony using a judo-type throw, but he didn't have his balance positioned properly. To compensate for his lack of leverage, Wade tried to out-muscle Tony. Tony was not the fastest wrestler in his class or the most knowledgeable about wrestling moves; however, he was extremely strong. He drove straight into Wade, knocking him backwards off his feet. Wade managed to twist his body in midair allowing him to land face down on the mat as opposed to on his back, and a split-second later Tony landed on top of him. Tony immediately slid his right forearm underneath Wade's right armpit and up and over the back of Wade's neck creating a half-nelson hold. Using this hold as a prybar, Tony forced Wade onto his back. Not surprisingly, when Wade's back touched the mat, he immediately arched up onto his head into a bridge position to keep his shoulders off the mat. To counter Wade's bridge, Tony kept his weight directly on top of Wade's chest as he tightened his right arm around the back of Wade's neck to complete the half-nelson pinning combination. This made it difficult for Wade to bridge up onto his head. After Tony held Wade on his back for over a minute, Wade's strength gave out and he dropped his shoulders to the mat. The referee slapped the mat signifying the fall.

I will never forget when the referee raised Tony's hand to indicate his victory, seeing our fans bolt out of the bleachers and sweep Tony off his feet. They carried him on their shoulders around the gymnasium three times showing everyone in the gym that Tony was their champion. Tony had not only taken first place in his weight class, but his win clinched the team title for our school. The quiet kid who was considered the underdog in the final, critical match of his home-town tournament ended up being the high school hero.

It has been many years since Tony won that wrestling tournament, but his victory is as clear in my mind as if it happened yesterday. Ever since that day, I have always tried to expect the absolute best out of anyone I managed. You never know when a person will exceed your expectations. Sometimes he/she just needs someone (or maybe a team) to believe in them.

Listen to Your Instincts

Each summer between college semesters my brother Ted helped me get hired as a laborer with whichever construction company he worked for at the time.[7] On the night before I started each job Ted would say to me "Just work hard, Tim and you'll do fine." On the first work day during my fourth summer, I was assigned to assist a laborer named Jack. Jack had spent many years working in the construction business. He was a tough, old guy with broad shoulders and a hand shake that informed you he was a force to be reckoned with. What made Jack look even tougher was his rather leathery face, most likely due to working outside in the sun for many years.

Our assignment was to cut three, 16 by 16-inch holes into a concrete deck at the top of an elevator shaft in the Federal Center (a large government building in Battle Creek). Arriving at the building, we found the three squares marked off with blue tape. With a cigarette hanging out of the corner of his mouth, Jack began hammering out the first hole with an electric jackhammer. Meanwhile, I used a shovel to scoop up the broken concrete pieces

---

[7] The money I made from those summer jobs played a major role in financing my college education. I owe my brother for helping me to obtain my college degree.

and tossed them into a bin. As the size of the first hole grew, some of the debris fell through the hole into the elevator shaft. Directly below the concrete deck was a scaffold which had been temporarily installed in the shaft. Jack didn't want the debris to fall through the hole and create a mess on the scaffold so he instructed me to reach down and grab the loose pieces of concrete before they fell into the hole. Because this was my first day on the job and I wanted to make a good impression, I knelt down on my right knee and tried to reach for a chunk of debris. That's when a bizarre thing happened; I couldn't move my arm. It was as if an invisible hand was holding my arm and not letting it stretch forward to grab the loose chunk of concrete. As more pieces fell through the hole, Jack became agitated and snapped, "Boy, don't let any of those concrete pieces fall through that hole! Don't worry, I won't hurt you. I've got control of this hammer. Just grab those pieces of concrete as I break them free." But it didn't appear Jack had complete control of the jackhammer. The hammer's steel blade was erratically bouncing from one spot to another within the square marked off by the tape. As Jack continued to hammer, I attempted to reach for pieces of concrete, but my arm refused to cooperate. More pieces fell through the hole and Jack became angry. Then, just as Jack cursed, his jackhammer jerked to one side and the steel blade came down severing the jackhammer's own electric cord. Sparks flew and the hammer died. I realized if I had complied with Jack's demands, I could have easily lost my hand. An electrician nearby quickly repaired the cut cord and within few minutes Jack was hammering out the remainder of the holes. He didn't ask me to grab any more of the loose pieces of concrete. When Jack finished cutting out the last hole, I cleaned up the remaining debris on the deck and went down into the elevator shaft to gather up the rubble which had fallen onto the scaffold.

I'm not sure what was holding my arm back that day. It might have been a guardian angel or my subconscious or just plain old fear, but if you ever have a similar experience, I highly recommend you heed your intuition.

The Challenge

After graduating from college with a major in mathematics, a nearby school district hired me as a 9th grade math teacher. On the second day of classes our principle held an all-school assembly where he spoke about his vision for the coming year. Each teacher was assigned to sit with the students from their first-hour class.

As I sat down with my students, I spotted a paper-wad fly through the air a few rows in front of me and hit a student on the back of his head. When the student turned around, I saw it was Bobby Joe from my 4th hour class. A moment later, another paper-wad hit Bobby Joe. The shooter was obviously targeting Bobby Joe, a quiet soul who wouldn't retaliate. Based on the high rate of speed that the wads had traveled I assumed the shooter was using a rubber band to launch the paper-wads. When the third wad hit Bobby Joe, I was able to pinpoint the shooter. It was Kyle, a student in my 6th hour class. The teacher who was assigned to oversee the section of the auditorium where Kyle was sitting, was at the opposite end of Kyle's row and was unaware of his antics. I stood up and walked down the aisle to the end of Kyle's row. He was sitting five seats in and since I couldn't see the rubber band, nor could I speak to him without raising my voice and causing a scene, I just glared at him. Realizing he was caught, Kyle slouched down into his seat and stared into his lap.

A couple of minutes later, the assembly began. Instead of going back to my seat, I stepped back and leaned against the wall so as to keep an eye on Kyle and to make sure he didn't shoot any more paper-wads. When I looked across the auditorium, I spotted Mr. Jackson, the assistant principle. He was staring at me while standing in a classic defensive linebacker stance as if he was ready to rush forward if needed. I smiled and nodded my head. Mr. Jackson's face changed from a stern look to a smile and he nodded back. He relaxed his posture, turned and walked to another part of the auditorium. After the assembly ended, Mr. Jackson met me at the exit door and asked what was going on before the assembly started. I told him about Kyle and the paper-wads. He thanked me for intervening and said he would speak to Kyle.

The following was relayed to me by the office secretary:

Later that morning, Mr. Jackson was standing outside his office when he spotted Kyle and asked him to come into his office for a moment.

Mr. Jackson: "Kyle, I'd like you to empty your pockets and place whatever you have in them on my desk."

Kyle reached into his front jean pockets and pulled a dollar bill from one pocket and an eraser from the other pocket. He dropped both items onto Mr. Jackson's desk.

Mr. Jackson: "Now I'd like you to reach into your front pockets again, but this time pull them inside out."

Kyle slowly reached into his front pockets and pulled them inside out.

Mr. Jackson: "Open your hands and place their contents on my desk."

Kyle opened his hands and dropped two rubber bands and several paper-wads onto the desk.

Mr. Jackson: "Thank you, Kyle. You can come into the office tonight after school and spend an hour thinking about your conduct in today's assembly."

Kyle: "I can't come tonight. I have football practice."

Mr. Jackson: "Oh, I think you can come tonight and you will if you want to stay on the team."

Kyle: "This isn't fair! You can't make me miss practice just because I have some rubber bands in my pocket!"

Mr. Jackson: "You should have thought of that this morning before you pelted Bobby Joe with paper-wads during our assembly."

Kyle, who was unaware of Mr. Jackson's past blurted out, "You just don't care about our football team! In fact, you don't care about any of our teams! All you care about are the stupid rules in this stupid school."

Kyle's last statement must have struck a nerve with Mr. Jackson. He had spent decades coaching every sport the school had to offer including football so kids like Kyle could have the opportunity to play. Mr. Jackson paused for a moment, then said, "Because you're such an important player on the team, I'll give you an alternative. We'll arm wrestle. If you win, you can go to practice tonight. If I win, you come here after school and miss practice."

Kyle stood the same height as Mr. Jackson. He looked the assistant principal in the eye and the corners of his mouth turned up ever so slightly to form a smile as he said, "Sure, I'll arm wrestle you."

Kyle was looking at a man who was one year away from retiring. The small amount of hair left on Mr. Jackson's head had turned white and the lenses in his glasses were as thick as pop-bottle glass. Mr. Jackson also had numerous lines etched into his face from the challenges of keeping order and discipline in the school for decades. Kyle smiled as he placed his elbow on the desk and clasped Mr. Jackson's hand.

Mr. Jackson spoke, "On three: one, two, three."

Wham! The back of Kyle's hand hit the top of Mr. Jackson's desk so fast it caused Kyle's mouth to gape in disbelief. What Kyle had failed to notice about Mr. Jackson was that beneath his sport coat was a barrel chest and huge biceps which had been developed and maintained by lifting weights ever since he played sports in high school as a teenager.

Mr. Jackson spoke one last time, “I’ll see you here at 3:00 o’clock sharp this afternoon. Oh, and you better let Coach Mason know you won’t be at practice tonight and make sure you tell him why you won’t be there.”

You should never underestimate your opponent, even when he is fifty years older than you.

Honesty Is the Best Policy

Many years ago, my wife and I were taking our two-year-old daughter Katie to see Lori's parents. We had just left our home when Katie asked, "Mommy, do you have my PJs?" Lori replied, "Yes, they're in your travel bag." Katie waited a few minutes before saying, "I want blanky." Lori reached to get Katie's blanket out of the travel bag, but Katie interrupted saying, "I get it! I get it!" Lori handed the travel bag to her and upon looking into it, Katie asked, "Where my PJs?" I laughed and said to Lori, "You were just outsmarted by a two-year-old. Katie didn't want her blanket when she asked for it, she just wanted to see if her pajamas were in the travel bag as you had told her. Heaven help us when she becomes a teenager!"

It is always best to tell the truth, especially when you are dealing with a two-year-old who is smarter than you. However, there is one exception. When the two-year-old becomes a five-year-old and she asks you, "Is there really a Santa Claus?", tell her to ask her other parent.

The Advantages of Being a Wrestler

My first high-tech job sent me to Portland, Oregon for three weeks to attend a training class. It was an intense class and my classmates and I were overwhelmed by the barrage of new technical information we received each day. Consequently, when class ended on the first Friday, all of us went to dinner to celebrate the successful completion of the first week. The dinner went well until we left the restaurant and realized George, our driver, had too much to drink.

George was a nice guy and I had become friends with him during the training sessions. However, when we tried to coax him into giving us the car keys, he refused and became belligerent. We instinctively formed a circle around him in the parking lot to prevent him from getting into the car. Unfortunately for me, I was the one standing between George and the car. As he tried to push me out of the way I resisted. To my surprise, he slapped me across the face and kneed me in the groin. Losing his balance, George stumbled backwards and laughed. I was stunned how a few drinks had so quickly changed George's personality from Dr. Jekyll to Mr. Hyde. Luckily, George was so inebriated that neither of his blows harmed me.

At this point in my life, I had several high school classmates who had died in car accidents while driving under the influence of alcohol. George's actions galvanized my determination to not let him drive us back to the hotel. There were no street fighters in our group. We were just a bunch of technical nerds who liked to learn about computers and George was our leader by default because he was the tallest and most gregarious. George attempted to break out of our circle by pushing and slapping others while laughing. I stepped into the inner circle and spoke, "George, I need the car keys."

George turned and replied: "You need the car keys?"

Me: "Yes, I need the car keys."

George: "I'll show you what you need!"

George stood six-feet tall and towered over me, but I had one clear advantage. I had a background in wrestling which neither he nor anyone in the group knew. As George swung his fist, I ducked, grabbed his swinging arm and pulled it down tight to my body as I rolled George across my shoulders using a fireman-carry takedown. It was George's misfortune that he had never been a wrestler because a wrestler would have instinctively tucked into a ball and rolled across the pavement. Instead, George's face slammed into the asphalt, knocking him momentarily unconscious. As he laid on his back, I pulled the car keys from his pocket.

Larry spoke: "Should we pick him up and help him get into the car?"

Me: "Not yet! It's better to wait and see if he can stand up on his own. That will give us an indication that he isn't hurt too badly."

After a few minutes, George rolled onto his stomach and slowly got on his hands and knees. He wavered there for a minute and then stood up. Larry and the others helped George into the backseat of the car. As I walked toward the driver's side door, Sandy stepped in front of me and spoke, "I need the car keys!"

Me: "I'm fine. I can drive us back to the hotel."

Sandy: "Do you also need to be flipped onto the pavement?"

She had a valid point so I handed her the car keys and got into the car via the front passenger door. Sandy, who had not been drinking, drove us safely back to the hotel.

The sport of wrestling gave me many skills besides the ability to wrestle. It taught me how hard work and determination pays off. It also gave me several friendships that have lasted over my lifetime. After considering what occurred during that night in Portland, both my new friends and I might well owe our lives to my ability to wrestle.

Many years have passed since that night and my days for executing a fireman-carry takedown have long passed. Thus, to be honest, if

I were to encounter the same situation today, I would just call a taxi.

Not to be Trifled With

Lori, our kids and I had been living in Cleveland, Ohio for three years when I was offered a promotion to a senior systems analyst position. As with any opportunity, there was a trade-off. We had to relocate to the company's regional office in Dallas, Texas, placing us 1,000 miles away from our families. After discussing the pros and cons, we agreed it was too good of an opportunity to pass up.

A few weeks later, after a moving van had taken our furniture, we drove to Dallas and found our hotel room didn't contain a kitchenette. Even though we were worn out from our travels, I suggested we go out to dinner—I should have known better!

At the restaurant we saw my new, second-level manager who was with one of his friends. We spoke to them for a minute before being seated by the waitress. As I mentioned, we were all very tired. We had eaten barely half our dinner when our kids began to fuss. Hurriedly, we had the remainder of our dinner boxed up and headed for the exit door. As we passed my second-level manager and his friend, Lori noticed they were looking at us and smirking. Since Lori has never been one to be easily intimidated, she looked them in the eye and said, "You aren't laughing at us, ARE YOU?"

Both of these hotshots wiped the grins off their faces so fast that you would've thought Lori had slapped them. They promptly replied, "No ma'am!", "No ma'am!" Lori smiled, signaling that she was kidding and responded, "Good!"

Here I was starting a new job over 1,000 miles from our hometown and my wife let my new boss's boss know she was not one to be trifled with. You have to love her! I guess that is one of the many reasons why I married her. She is not afraid to speak what is on her mind.

Trust

I was on my way to the Fort Worth hospital to bring Lori and our newborn daughter home when all of a sudden steam started pouring out from under the car hood. I pulled off the freeway and confirmed the leak was from a small split in the radiator hose. Fortunately, I had learned from a previous experience to always carry duct tape in my car for such occasions[8]. After wrapping tape around the opening in the hose, I started the car and confirmed the tape had sealed the leak shut. I continued on to the hospital. Fortuitously, I spotted a car parts store after exiting the freeway and stopped to purchase a new hose before continuing on to the hospital.

I approached the clerk who was standing behind the counter. "What can I do for you?" the clerk asked. I pointed to my car in the parking lot and replied, "I need a radiator hose for that 1984 Cavalier." The clerk checked his parts manual, wrote down a part number and pulled a hose from a shelf.

Clerk: "That'll be ten dollars."

---

[8] See *Who Said That?*

I reached into my wallet and found only a five-dollar bill. Debit cards did not exist back then and I didn't have my credit card with me.

I placed the five-dollar bill on the counter and said, "I only have five bucks on me. Can I bring you the other five tomorrow morning?"

Clerk: "Sure, and then I'll sell you the hose!"

Me: "Seriously, I'll be back first thing in the morning with the other five bucks."

Clerk: "And then I'll sell you the hose!"

Luckily, there were no other customers in the store so the clerk didn't have a reason to tell me to step aside. At this point in my life, I really didn't like to debate due to my inability to think fast and explain myself under pressure; normally, I would have just left, but this was one of those rare times where I stood my ground and said:

> "Buddy, I'm on my way to pick up my wife and newborn daughter at the hospital. My radiator hose has a leak and is being held together with duct tape. I can't risk that hose splitting apart while I'm driving them home on the freeway to Euless. I'll be back tomorrow morning with the other five bucks."

I continued to stand at the counter while the two of us stared each other down. After what seemed like an eternity, the clerk pushed the hose to my side of the counter and said, “We open at 9:00 a.m.”

Me: “Thank you! I’ll be here when you open!”

After replacing the damaged hose, I proceeded to the hospital.

I was sitting in my car the next morning when the same clerk from the previous day unlocked the store door. I entered the store, stepped up to the counter and handed him a five-dollar bill. He grinned broadly and said, “I was pretty sure I wasn’t ever going to see you again.”

I just smiled and thanked him for trusting me.

After that incident I learned to always carry my credit card. More importantly, I just want to thank that clerk in Texas again. Thank you for trusting a total stranger who promised to pay you in full for that hose so many years ago.

The Gray Falcon

Thanksgiving is one of my favorite holidays. We eat all kinds of delicious foods and we typically have friends and family come over to watch parades and football games. During our first year in Texas, we had no one to invite because we hadn't developed any close friendships. To compensate for a lack of company, I created a treasure hunt for our children. I wrote six separate clues on small pieces of paper. To make each clue look very old and easy to identify, I burned the edges. Each clue was signed, "The Gray Falcon." The first clue was hidden in my son's favorite toy which he found early Thanksgiving morning. Because Tyler couldn't read yet, he took the clue to his older sister. After reading the clue, Katie jumped up and hollered, "It's a clue to a treasure hunt!" Each clue led the treasure seekers to their next clue until they found the treasure—gold, wrapped, chocolate coins.

The hunt was an enormous success and I promptly forgot about it until a year later when I came home from work on Thanksgiving eve. As I entered our home, Lori mentioned that our kids were in the backyard playing Gray Falcon and there had better be a treasure hunt the next morning, or we were going to have some pretty unhappy children. I immediately went to the store and purchased more gold, wrapped, chocolate coins.

This was the beginning of a tradition in our family which has lasted many years. As my children grew older, the hunt became more challenging and required them to use new skills they had learned during the previous school year. For example, when Tyler was a boy scout, he learned Morse code so at least one clue from that hunt going forward was written in Morse code. A year later, one of my daughters had a school lesson on how to read braille. Thus, one of the clues was written in braille. Another year, one of the clues was encoded in hieroglyphics and a second clue was written in ASCII binary character format. The treasure hunters also had to learn how to read a compass because some of the clues required them to hunt for the next clue in a particular direction. The treasure hunts eventually moved to a local park where the clues were found in trees, swing sets and other places.

The climactic hunt occurred when Katie was in college and Tyler, Alexa and Shoshi were in high school, middle school, and elementary school respectively. The first clue was found in our house two-days before Thanksgiving. It included three bus tickets departing the next day to Eugene, Oregon. This first clue instructed the three younger kids to take the family cell phone, their backpacks, sleeping bags and treasure-hunting tools, such as decoders for Morse code, braille, hieroglyphics and ASCII binary characters. Katie had a class when the bus was due to arrive in Eugene so she asked her roommate (whom my kids had never met) to meet her siblings. This added an extra element of excitement.

The first clue only told the siblings they would be met in Eugene by a person wearing a hat with a sunflower on it.

Katie fully embraced the challenge as the Gray Falcon and she guided her siblings as they traipsed all over campus searching for clues in the college library, stadium, parks and other places while neither my wife nor I were present. Katie made a marvelous Gray Falcon!

When I originally planned the first treasure hunt, its only purpose was to provide my children with a fun activity on Thanksgiving Day. Over time the treasure hunts grew to be far more than simply a game. It taught my children many non-traditional skills, such as how to read a compass or how to solve a problem by decoding a message. More importantly, my children learned how to work together as a team so they could depend on each other when needed in the future.

The role of the Gray Falcon has since been passed on to my children who now create the treasure hunts for their own children on Thanksgiving Day.

May the Gray Falcon live on forever!

Be Careful of The Tricks You Teach Your Kids

Children Are Always Listening

I used to play a game with my children when they were young called fly-like-superman. I would lie on my back, pull my knees up to my chest and have one of the kids sit on my feet. I would then boost them into the air and catch them before they came down. I know, this sounds dangerous! It was dangerous as I learned one night.

I was in the shower when my wife came running into the bathroom to tell me our three-year-old, Alexa, had broken her arm. She had tried to play the fly-like-superman game with her older brother, but Tyler was only five and didn't realize he was supposed to catch her. I hurriedly put on a T-shirt, jeans and tennis shoes and went to examine Alexa's arm. Lori's diagnosis was correct. Alexa's forearm was clearly broken as was evident by a kink in her arm above the wrist.

I wrapped a magazine around the broken forearm and tied two bandanas around it to create a splint that would prevent the arm from moving and being damaged more severely. I carefully loaded Alexa into the back seat of our van. In the meantime, Lori had our next-door neighbor come over to watch the other three children while we rushed Alexa to the hospital. Alexa quieted down during the ride and seemed to fall asleep while Lori and I spoke quietly so as to not wake her. To break the tension of the moment, I mentioned I was in such a rush getting dressed that I didn't put on any underwear. This made Lori laugh.

When we got to the hospital, Alexa was amazingly calm considering her injury. The nurse asked us how Alexa broke her arm and after we answered the question, she asked Alexa the same question. The nurse was obviously double-checking our story. To my surprise, instead of answering the nurse's question, Alexa looked at me and asked, "Daddy, why you not have any panties on?"

I was caught by surprise and didn't know how to reply in front of the nurse who was now staring at me with a curious look on her face. I began imagining what this nurse might be thinking, such as, "How does this three-year-old girl know that her father isn't wearing any underwear?" or "Does this guy really wear panties?"

Because I hadn't responded immediately, Alexa appeared to think I hadn't heard her so she said it again, only louder, "Daddy, why you not have any panties on?"

I replied, "I was in such a hurry rushing you to the hospital that I didn't have time to put on my underwear."

For the nurse's benefit I asked Alexa to describe how she broke her arm, which she did. The nurse walked away and a few minutes later she returned with a doctor who also asked Alexa how she broke her arm. Finally, after both the nurse and doctor concluded that no foul play had occurred, they X-rayed the arm, set it, wrapped it in a cast and sent us home.

Alexa was very brave that night. Her arm healed and I learned a couple of valuable lessons. First, never play a game with your children that you don't want them to play when you are not present. Secondly, when your child asks you an embarrassing question in front of other people, answer it immediately, unless you want her to repeat it only louder so everyone in the room can hear it.

Premonition

Upon arriving home after running a few errands on a Saturday morning in Texas, I noticed that both Katie's and Tyler's bikes weren't in the garage. This was not unusual for a Saturday since Katie was eleven and Tyler was nine, but something didn't seem right. I got out of the van and looked up and down the street. Seeing no sign of them, I stepped into our house and called, "Lori, I'm home. Where are Katie and Tyler?"

Lori: "They're out riding their bikes."

Me: "How long have they been gone?"

Lori: "They've been gone about an hour. Why?"

Me: "I don't know, but something seems wrong."

Lori: "What seems wrong?"

Me: "I don't know, but I'm going to go look for them."

I stepped outside and looked up and down the street again without seeing any sign of them. At this point my stomach began to tighten and I had this feeling my kids were in danger. It's not like I heard a voice or had a vision. I just had a bad feeling. I climbed back into the van and started to drive over to one of Katie's friend's house.

On the way, I passed a small park called Bear Creek Park. I stopped, turned the van around and drove into the park. As I scanned the landscape, I spotted my kids' bikes on the far side of the park next to a gully. The gully was about six-feet deep and it routed the creek through the park. From where I was sitting, I couldn't see the creek or my children and my heart began to race. I felt a sense of anxiety sweep over me as I stepped out of the van and started jogging toward the creek. With each step I took my pace sped up until I was at a full sprint. When I reached the edge of the gully, I could see both Katie and Tyler below in the creek. Katie was hip deep in the water standing over Tyler who must have been sitting because his head was the only portion of him above the water line. I called out, "Katie!" She turned, and upon seeing me she yelled back, "I can't get him out of the creek! He's stuck!" I jumped into the gully and waded into the water towards them. When I reached Tyler, I stooped down, wrapped my arms around him and tried to lift him out of the water. I immediately understood what Katie had said. Tyler was truly stuck in the muddy creek! His shoes had sunk several inches into the creek bed and they wouldn't move. It was as if they were cemented in place. I spoke to Katie, "Take your bike and go home. I'll take care of Tyler." She climbed out of the gully, got on her bike and rode home. I have to give Katie credit for wading into the cold, muddy creek in an attempt to free her brother from his entrapment.

I glanced up at the sky to confirm it was clear and there was no sign of rain. This part of the country was known for having flash floods and a creek's water level could rise a couple of feet within a very short time. Fortunately, the sky was clear; however, I did say a quick prayer that there weren't any stray alligators or even worse, water moccasins nearby.

I knelt down in the water and stood Tyler up. While holding him steady with one arm, I dug around both sides of Tyler's left shoe. It took a minute to free his shoe because it was submerged several inches into the creek bed. Next, I dug around the other shoe. When I finally freed both shoes, I picked him up and carried him out of the creek. I was relieved that it only took a couple of minutes to free him because my own shoes had sunk a couple of inches into the muck and it took effort to break free.

We were both soaked, covered with mud and Tyler was shivering from being in the cold water. I carried him to the van and then went back and got his bike. When we arrived home, I rinsed the mud off both of us with the outside hose before taking Tyler into the house where I put him in a warm bath. It was at this point my heart finally stopped racing.

This was the only time I had ever experienced such a powerful premonition. To this day I can't believe how strong of an alarm feeling I had for my children without having any evidence of a problem. Something just told me I had to find them immediately and I'm thankful I responded when I did.

In summary, if you ever have such a feeling, act on it immediately. Don't wait!

Use Your Requests Wisely

Typically, a person has a limited number of requests he/she can ask of someone before the person will start ignoring the request. The following are some additional observations:

1. The more requests you ask of someone (who doesn't work for you) the less likely he or she will be willing to assist you. Unless you can repay a person in some manner, use your requests wisely.
2. To increase the odds of getting a request fulfilled, stack the deck ahead of time by assisting others with their requests.
3. Because of their charisma or position in society, some people can make more requests and have them met than others can.

The following story provides insight on how I learned about requests.

When I was a systems analyst, one of my managers was Anne. She often called me concerning major customer issues. She would ask me to contact the customer and address the concern. At the end of each phone call she would ask, "Is there anything I can do to help?" I would always tell her, "No, I'll take care of the issues right away."

After working for Anne for several months, she held a team meeting in California to plan strategies for the upcoming year. At the end of the first day, several of us met in the hotel lounge to discuss the results of the day. The team decided Anne should join us and I was selected to invite her to the lounge.

All of us knew my assignment was going to be a challenge since Anne didn't typically hang out in the hotel lounge. When I knocked on her door, she didn't open it. Instead, she asked through the closed door what I needed. I told her our team was requesting her presence for a team-building discussion. She responded that she was done working for the evening and wouldn't be able to attend. I paused for a moment to consider how I would phrase my next few words and then said, "I have a question."

Anne: "What's your question?"

Me: "Whenever you call me, what is the last thing you say to me?"

Anne: "Hmm, I don't remember."

Me: "You always ask me, 'Is there anything I can do to help?'"

Anne: "Okay."

Me: "And what do I say to you?"

Anne: "I don't remember."

Me: "I always tell you, 'No, I'll take care of the issue.'"

Me: “Do you agree?”

Anne: “Yes.”

Me: “Well I’m asking you for some help now. Our team has requested you come to the lounge to participate in one more discussion tonight.”

Anne thought for a moment and replied, “You drive a hard bargain, Tim Kellogg. I’ll be down in 15 minutes, but I think you should transfer into sales.”

In summary, be careful about asking for help unless you truly need it.

Life Is Like a Chess Game

When I mention to people that my family and I used to live in Texas, they sometimes ask, “Why did you leave?” I typically tell them the following story about a football game that my wife and I attended.

We had been in Texas for six years and it was an October evening when Lori and I went to a high school football game. We both wore jeans because we always wore jeans when attending football games in Michigan where it was considerably cooler. Unfortunately, the temperature that night was 90°F and it was about halfway through the game when Lori turned to me and said, “That’s it! If I can’t wear jeans to a football game, I’m not staying in Texas!” She then laughed, hinting that she was kidding or maybe half kidding. Even though this story is true, the real reason we left Texas is a little more complicated.

At this point in my career, I was a consulting systems analyst in the sales department for a high-tech company. My position was also referred to as second-level support because I normally didn’t deal directly with our customers. Instead, I primarily trained the other systems analysts who in turn assisted our customers with system issues. Sadly, our division had been struggling and there had been multiple layoffs during the past couple of years.

On a fateful day, I received a call from the sales manager who informed me there was another layoff and the division was eliminating all second-level positions. He then offered me a first-level position. Regrettably, if I were to accept this position, it would cause my friend Dan to be laid off instead of me. The sales manager also said he needed my answer by 5:00 pm that day.

It was very generous of my manager to offer me the other position; however, I had been working with Dan for the past six years and he had a stellar reputation for solving problems and helping customers. I had seen this type of offer made by other managers in the past so I was prepared for it. I thanked my manager for the offer and informed him I wouldn't be taking the other position. Dan had a wife and a newborn son and I had no desire to take his job.

It may appear that my response was rash considering my family and I were primarily living off of my salary, but it wasn't a rash decision. For the previous couple of years, I had saved a small amount of money from each paycheck. This was very challenging since there were always more needs than money for a family of six. Fortunately, we now had a small reserve and the job market was fairly good. In fact, I recently had a job offer from another company so I didn't feel the need to take a job that would cause

Dan to lose his job. As it turned out, I ended up staying with that company and taking a training manager position in Oregon.

It's best to observe all events occurring around you. Whatever ills befall a coworker may someday happen to you.

Life is like a chess game; you have to always be looking ahead and be prepared for what fate might throw at you.

Things Aren't Always What They Seem

My first task as a training manager was to oversee the staff's creation of a self-study guide to upgrade the company's technicians' software skills. Their current skills were focused on repairing customers' printers which were connected to PCs. The purpose of the new guide was to broaden the technicians' understanding of the common commands and applications executed on a PC. This allowed them to troubleshoot a wider range of problems and generate more revenue for the service department.

Besides developing the self-study guide, my team also had to create a test for each technician to pass. The service managers didn't have time to proctor these tests so they were issued using an honor system. This concerned me, but it was the only available method at the time. We mailed the new self-study guide and test to each technician in the field. They were instructed to return their test answers on a floppy disk.

The directions for taking the test were as follows:

1. Write your name on the outside label of the floppy disk.
2. Format the floppy disk.
3. Create a file on the floppy disk and name the file "Answers."

4. Enter your name on the first line in the file.
5. Enter one answer per line for each multiple-choice test question.

The technicians sent their floppy disks back to my secretary who graded the tests.

This process went well for the first couple of weeks until my secretary asked me to review a couple of disks which had arrived from the New Jersey service center. One disk was from a technician named Mark, and the other from a technician named Paul. My secretary listed the contents from Mark's floppy disk and everything seemed appropriate. Mark had only missed question #12 out of the 50 questions. My secretary ejected Mark's disk from her PC and inserted Paul's disk. She then listed the contents of Paul's file which were identical to the contents of Mark's file, including Mark's name being on the first line of Paul's file. It appeared that Paul had copied Mark's disk. I called Paul's and Mark's manager and explained what we found. I was careful not to accuse either technician of doing anything unethical. I just stated the facts. Their manager thanked me and said he would address the issue.

I felt uneasy about the entire situation. I just couldn't believe that Paul would be so careless as to copy Mark's disk and not bother to replace Mark's name with his own name in the file. Paul must not have read the test directions carefully, or he would have known that Mark's name was in the file.

The next morning, I inserted Paul's floppy disk into my PC's disk drive and listed his test answers. To my surprise, Paul's name was on the first line in his file, which was not what I had observed the previous day and he had only missed question #32. I felt like I was entering the Twilight Zone! I ejected Paul's disk from the PC, inserted Mark's disk and listed the contents of his file. This time Paul's name was at the top of Mark's file and Mark's answers were identical to Paul's answers which was the opposite of what I had observed the previous day. Then it occurred to me what was happening. When the operating system examined the directory of the second disk, which was just inserted into the drive, and saw that the disk's directory was identical to the first disk which had just been ejected (only one file was present and its filename was "Answers"), the operating system assumed the same floppy disk had been reinserted into the disk drive. To save time displaying the information, the operating system listed the contents of the file from its RAM memory without rereading the contents of the file from the second floppy disk. This led me to believe that Paul had unethically copied Mark's disk, when in reality nothing unethical had occurred. I immediately called Mark's and Paul's manager to explain what I had discovered and to offer my apology. He was very gracious and said he hadn't yet spoken to either technician so we could drop the issue. I thanked him.

This experience taught me not to jump to conclusions, especially when a situation doesn't make sense. Instead, I should take time to investigate any possible circumstances that may have been overlooked.

I also learned that whenever I have a misunderstanding with another person, I should always treat that person with dignity and respect and listen carefully with an open mind because no matter how much proof I have that I am correct, there is always the possibility I might still be wrong.

Lessons We Learn from Our Children

I've learned many lessons from my children over the years and one of the more important lessons learned was from my youngest daughter Shoshi.

When Shoshi was in high school, she was diagnosed with scoliosis, an irregular shaped curvature of the spine. To address this curve, Shoshi endured two major surgeries within a four-year period. These surgeries did not prevent Shoshi from wanting to compete in sports. After healing from the second surgery, she told her mother and me that she was going to run on the high school's cross-country team. I was very concerned for Shoshi's health, but she was determined she was ready. We checked with her doctor and he gave his approval, yet I still had concerns. My wife let me know I was being overly protective. With Shoshi's doctor's approval, and my wife's influence, I reluctantly agreed to let Shoshi run on the school's cross-country team.

Shoshi's first cross-country season was extremely challenging. Her surgeries left her in less-than-optimum running condition. This was demonstrated in each race by her typically being one of the last runners to finish the race, but this did not deter her. She finished the season and went out for cross-country again the following year and with each race, Shoshi's performance improved. Several coaches from other teams, who had watched Shoshi during the previous season, congratulated her on her improvement and told her she was an inspiration to them. More than one of these coaches said to her, "I wish some of my own runners had as much determination as you."

At the end of Shoshi's final cross-country season, the coach presented her with an award for her tenacity and perseverance.

The determination and persistence that Shoshi demonstrated through sports has served her well in pursuing other life goals. Lori and I have always been very proud of our daughter and her commitment to pursuing her dreams.

Skills and ability will take a person a long way, but determination and hard work can take them even further.

Karma – Part 2

I had just left home and was driving to work one morning when I spotted red and white colored clothes in the street. I veered around the clothes in order to not damage them and then stopped to move them out of the street. The clothes were a nice pair of pajamas; they appeared to have been accidently dropped when the owner was in a hurry going to either school or work. I picked up the pajamas and draped them over a nearby tree branch to protect them from other cars running over them. I continued on to work. In the evening when I returned, the pajamas were gone and I assumed the owner had found them.

The following weekend my wife and I were at a high school cross-country invitational watching Shoshi race. It was a huge invitational and there were hundreds of parents, students and fans scattered all around the race route. As the front runners headed toward the finish line, Lori and I started walking to meet Shoshi when she finished. As we approached the finish line, Lori realized she had dropped her favorite denim blouse—she had hung it over her purse while walking. I backtracked in search of the blouse while Lori continued on ahead. I have to admit I was not optimistic about finding the blouse, let alone its condition because I assumed it had been trampled by the horde of spectators. Amazingly, after back tracking for a few minutes, I spotted the blouse. To my surprise it wasn't on the ground. Instead, it was draped over a tree branch in perfectly good condition just as I had left the pajamas two weeks earlier. Karma was paying me back!

Some people will tell you they don't believe in karma because they have never observed it, but I think it is because they haven't been paying attention. We just need to look to find it.

International Travel

The purpose of my first trip to Europe was to present new product training to my company's European sales force. I flew to Cologne, Germany with a few of the company's marketing staff and upon arrival we went out to dinner. After dinning at a beer hall, we decided to call it a night and started walking back to our hotel. It took us a while to find the street where the hotel was located, but strangely, after walking up and down the street, we couldn't find our hotel. We ended up going into another beer hall before resuming our search. By some miracle, we eventually found our hotel and slept for a few hours.

The training sessions went well. We gave our last presentation on Friday and decided to take a road trip the next day since our flight home didn't depart until Sunday. We toured a couple of medieval castles and visited a few quaint villages. In one of the villages, we paused at an intersection to watch a parade march past us. It was at this point my friend Shawn pointed to a street sign and said, "Check out the name of this street." After glancing at it, I said, "It's the same name as the street where our hotel is located back in Cologne." Shawn replied, "Yes, but look at the street name for the cross street." When I looked, I noticed a peculiar situation. The street names for the two intersecting streets were the same. I asked,

"How can the names for two intersecting streets be the same?" Shawn playfully cuffed me across the back of my head and using a pretend broken German accent said, "Silly American, Einbahnstraße means one-way street." It was a humbling experience and it taught me to always be able to identify a one-way street sign prior to visiting any foreign country so I wouldn't mistakenly search for my hotel on a street named, "One Way."

I found that with each country I visited, I would leave a little more humbled than when I arrived. For example, after visiting Europe my company purchased a reseller in Australia whose new responsibility was to sell our products in the South Pacific. I was asked to train the new sales force on the product line so I flew from Portland to Sydney with Dave, a company product manager. The first night in Sydney, we were scheduled to meet in the hotel restaurant with the CEO of the company that had been acquired. When I entered the restaurant, I noticed Dave hadn't arrived, but the CEO and some of his sales people were already sitting at a table. After introducing myself to the group, the CEO said to me in his thick Australian accent, "So you're an important person?" I was caught off guard since I didn't consider myself an important person. In this type of situation, I typically repeat the question so as to confirm what I thought the person said, "Am I an important person?"

Everyone at the table burst out laughing. When the CEO was able to stop laughing, he said, "Heck, I know you are an important person; otherwise, Dave wouldn't have brought you here." He then added, "I said, 'Are you a Portland person?'" All I could do was smile and reply, "Yes, I am a Portland person."

The best advice I can give to anyone who is about to visit a foreign country for the first time is to realize it will be a learning experience. It's better to not think too highly of yourself because you are most likely going to be embarrassed at some point during your visit.

Where's My Son?

My wife has seven younger siblings; she played a major role in raising them during her childhood. When she was only twelve years old she would get up in the middle of the night, heat up a bottle of formula and feed it to her baby sister to give her mother the chance to get a good night's rest. I didn't have any younger siblings; consequently, I was fairly inexperienced when it came to raising children. Due to this lack of experience, I'd have to say I was overly protective of my kids. Both my wife and my now-grown children will confirm this.

One example is a habit I had that neither my wife nor my kids knew about. For many years, whenever I woke in the middle of the night, I would go to the doorway of each of the kid's bedrooms and listen to their breathing. I just wanted to make sure they were okay. This ritual always set my mind at ease, allowing me to get back to sleep. One night, when my son Tyler was a sophomore in high school, I went to his doorway around 3:00 am and couldn't hear him breathing. Panic ensued and I rushed to his bedside. When I went to grab him, there was no one there, just a pile of coats stuffed under his bedspread. I walked downstairs and found the kitchen door to the garage unlocked as well as the garage backdoor that led outside. Every night I locked both of these doors;

thus, it was obvious Tyler had left the house. This night occurred when cell phones were not as common as they are today. Tyler didn't have a cell phone so there was no way for me to contact him. At about this time Lori came downstairs.

Lori: "Why are you up?"

Me: "I'm waiting for our son to come home."

Her eyes opened wide and she said, "Tyler isn't home?"

I shook my head. Lori suggested I call our friends whose sons were Tyler's best friends. Reluctantly, I made the call. When the boys' mother picked up the phone, I asked her to check and see if Tyler was at her house. She graciously agreed to check. A couple of minutes later she returned and informed me that Tyler wasn't there. I apologized for waking her up and bid her good night. I then recommended to Lori that she go back to bed while I stayed up to wait for our son to come home. There was no sense in both of us losing sleep while waiting for Tyler.

I sat down in a kitchen chair and my mind drifted back to a time many years earlier when I was twelve years old. My friend Rob was staying overnight and around midnight we crawled out of my bedroom window onto the kitchen roof. Next, we climbed down a maple tree which grew next to my house. Rob and I ran around the neighborhood for about an hour trying to find something fun to do, but none of our friends were out which made sense since it was midnight. We finally became bored and went back to my house, climbed back up the tree and into my bedroom. Everything seemed to have gone well except for one minor detail. A neighbor spotted us running by his house and the next day just happened to mention it to one of my parents. I still remember the punishment I received for my behavior that night.

Meanwhile, back to Tyler's story: Around 5:30 am I heard a car slowly drive past our house, stop for a moment and then drive away. Next, I heard the door to the back of our garage open and close very quietly. I got up and stood near the kitchen door to the garage. The door opened very slowly. When Tyler peeked his head inside, he saw me looking him straight in the eye. He realized he had been caught.

I spoke. "Where have you been?"

Tyler: "Just driving around."

Me: "Did you stop at any place?"

Tyler: "No."

When I asked him who he was with, he replied he was with his girlfriend.

Me: "Did you do anything that I would find unacceptable?"

Tyler: "I smoked some cigarettes."

I paused for a moment, collected my thoughts and said, "Go get some sleep. We'll discuss this later." I struggled with determining Tyler's consequences for his actions. After all I had pulled a similar stunt when I was a kid. Later that morning, Lori and I discussed the situation and agreed upon the following:

- Because Tyler had acted contrary to our house rules, he had to do something positive to balance out his negative actions, such as volunteer for a good cause.
- Also, because he had smoked cigarettes which were bad for his health, he had to run two miles every weekday for the rest of the summer. And to make sure he ran those two miles every weekday I would run with him.
- Lastly, Lori insisted that if Tyler wanted to maintain a relationship with his girlfriend, she had to come to our house to talk about the incident.

Tyler followed through on all of the above. We both volunteered at our church and helped build a new sidewalk by digging the trench and laying the forms for the concrete. It was a positive experience for both of us. Thereafter, every Sunday when we walked on that sidewalk, it reminded me of the positive outcome which resulted from Tyler's escapade.

Tyler also ran two miles every weekday morning with me for the rest of the summer. As for his girlfriend, she came over during the week when I wasn't there and apologized to Lori. Lori explained why their actions were so unnerving to us parents. I don't believe Tyler ever left our house again during the middle of the night.

Sometimes the best response to a child not following the rules isn't punishment, but a required action that yields a positive result.

Negotiating – Example 1

After managing the training department for four years, I moved to a product marketing manager position where I launched several different types of high-tech products. Several of them were thin clients (A thin clients is basically a computer terminal that displays multiple windows where each window may display information from a different computer.)

The last thin client I introduced was an outstanding product. It displayed information four times faster than any of the previous products and all of our customers loved it, except for one. A medical center in the Midwest ordered 60 of the new thin clients. Unfortunately, this customer ordered these devices without first testing a demo unit with their application. Upon installing one of the new thin clients, the customer discovered it did not support the maximum number of colors required to properly display CAT scan images. Both our data sheet and our website clearly stated the number of colors supported. Nonetheless, to make this customer happy I opted to have the thin client software enhanced to support the additional colors. I asked Ken, who was one of our best engineers, to make the required software changes. A week later we posted the updated software on our website; thereby, allowing customers to download it.

A couple of weeks passed and the customer who had requested the enhancement called. He was extremely upset. He had downloaded the updated software and found an issue with it. When using the new additional color mode, erroneous vertical lines intermittently appeared on the screen. I understood how this could be a concern when viewing an X-ray or a CAT scan. Regrettably, Ken (the engineer who updated the software) had left the company. The initial dot-com bubble[9] was at its peak and software engineers were in high demand. My company was doing poorly; thus, Ken (and all but one of our other engineers) moved to other companies for higher pay. I contacted Ken, but he was too busy to come back and address the software problem. I checked with Dave, who was our only remaining engineer and he said, "Ken is the only engineer qualified to address the issue." I continued to get angry emails from the customer, but I had no method to address the problem. I offered to pay Ken four times the going rate for his help, but again, he replied that he was too busy with his new job. I was getting desperate to find a solution before I had a major public relations disaster. I asked Dave again to try and address the issue. He suggested I contact Cindy, who was one of our other former engineers, to come back and work on the problem. I asked, "Is Cindy familiar with the software routine that needs to be modified?"

---

[9] The dot-com bubble (also known as the Internet bubble) was a stock market bubble caused by excessive speculation of Internet-related companies in the late 1990s. This bubble drove up high-tech stock prices as well as salaries.

Dave: “No, but she and Ken are friends.”

Me: “How does that help us?”

Dave: “Ken might not have time to help us, but maybe he has time to help Cindy.

Me: “That’s a great idea!”

I called Cindy and asked her to come by one evening after her regular workday to address the software problem. She responded that the problem was in a branch of the software which was beyond her expertise. I told her that was okay because I was going to have Ken stop by to give her some tips. Whether or not she could resolve the problem I would pay her. Next, I called Ken and told him Cindy was going to work on the issue and asked him to come by for a couple of minutes to give her some advice. Ken agreed.

On the given night both Cindy and Ken showed up, Ken immediately took control of the keyboard and had the software change implemented within a few minutes. Ken and Cindy then talked for the next 30 minutes while they ran several tests to confirm the updated software addressed the issue and didn’t create any new ones. Ken left and I paid Cindy for her time as I had promised.

This story is an example of how to negotiate. Ken was a highly paid engineer and the extra money I offered him to address the software problem was of no value to him. I had to find something he valued. Getting a chance to talk with a friend was the solution.

In summary, in order to negotiate with someone who doesn't have the time or the inclination to assist you, identify what that person values/needs and find a way to provide it.

Empowering Your Child

I didn't have many rules for raising my children when they were young; however, as they entered the teenage years, I required them to pay a small portion of their extracurricular activity costs. Not a major portion, just enough for them to realize it was part of their own funds being invested in the endeavor.

When my kids became college age, this rule applied to tuition. I was fairly open to how they could address this requirement. For example, they could work jobs during the summer or during the school year to help pay for their portion of the costs. Also, if they received a scholarship then it would apply toward their tuition requirement. The following is a discussion I had with my daughter Alexa after her sophomore year of college. She was debating how to earn her portion of the tuition for the upcoming fall semester.

A few days after Alexa's spring term ended, we drove back to Monmouth, Oregon to pick up her remaining belongings. After packing the car with her things, we stopped to get lunch. Alexa seemed fairly agitated. She was scheduled to fly to Michigan within the next week and stay with cousins for the summer, yet she needed a summer job. Her uncle had communicated a couple of months earlier that he would help her find a summer job, but to this date, no job had been identified. Alexa had plenty of contacts in Oregon which could assist her in getting a job at home, but she really wanted to go to Michigan to spend time with her cousins. As we discussed the situation, it was obvious the weight of the job issue was overwhelming. She appeared ready to give up, cancel her flight and stay in Oregon for the summer. I had two options for addressing these concerns. I could let her off the hook and tell her if she didn't get a job in Michigan then I would cover all school costs in the fall. On the other hand, I could empower her to solve the problem herself. Each person is different and you have to consider whether he or she is ready to address the issue at hand. Alexa had always been a diligent student and a leader among her peers; therefore, I was confident she could find a job once arriving in Michigan.

I said, "Your uncle has lived in Michigan all his life and has numerous business contacts who will need help this summer. I'm certain he will help you find a job. However, if for some reason he doesn't, it's not a problem because you will find a job on your own and you will make this summer a success. You just need to get on that plane, fly to Michigan and figure things out once you land."

That said, Alexa's expression changed. It was as if I had lifted a huge weight off her shoulders.

She replied, "Okay, I'll go."

Alexa's uncle did help her find a summer job at a local swimming pool where she made enough money to pay for the upcoming fall tuition.

My view of parental responsibility was not to solve my kids' problems for them. Instead, I needed to empower and guide them so they could learn how to solve problems themselves.

Negotiating – Example 2

When I first became a product marketing manager, a wise mentor took me aside and said, "You will be asked to make all types of decisions in your new position. Some of these decisions will be easy, others will be difficult and you will not like the outcome." He added, "In such a scenario, stall and wait as long as you can before making the decision." The following is an example of such a situation.

After leaving the thin client business, I joined a company that developed and sold printers. My new role was to champion the printers during their development cycles as well as after they were introduced to the market. The company's research team had recently developed an easy-to-use graphical user interface (GUI) for changing colors on images before printing. This new GUI did not require the user to define a new color using the confusing color models like cyan, magenta and yellow ratios. Instead, the user simply specified the source color to change and its replacement color using four dropdown menus in the new GUI. For example, suppose a user had an image of a beautiful house, but the grass in the yard was all yellow. The user could change the color of the yellow grass to dark green by specifying a sentence using four menus, such as:

"Make All Yellow Dark Green."

The users didn't need to know how to mix the appropriate proportions of cyan, magenta and yellow to display the dark green color. The user just selected the desired color and its adjective from the lists in the dropdown menus. This new GUI would be a unique feature which would help differentiate our new printer from the competition.

Unfortunately, early in the upcoming printer's development cycle, one of the engineering managers came to me and said we had to drop the new GUI feature from the upcoming printer features. The key engineer required to write the new software was working on another higher-priority project and would not be available until after the printer's engineering-completion deadline had passed. "Is there any other engineer qualified to write the software?" I asked. Sadly, he replied, "No." I understood this manager's predicament. If he didn't have a qualified engineer available, he couldn't deliver the software on time which would delay the printer's introduction. But why make this decision at that time? Because the engineering-completion milestone for the upcoming printer was three months in the future, I managed to convince the engineering manager to wait and delay making the decision to eliminate the new GUI for at least a month.

A month later, at a project review meeting for the upcoming printer, I was told again we had to drop the new GUI from the printer's features. I asked, "Is there any software in the new GUI that another engineer could implement so when our key engineer becomes available, he could write the crucial software in less time?" The engineering manager replied, "Yes, there are some software libraries that need to be built and another engineer could build them."

The outcome of the meeting was the team's agreement to allow another engineer to build the software libraries. As a result, we delayed the decision to drop the new GUI again. Three weeks later, after the required libraries had been built, the engineering manager came to me on a Monday and said the key engineer had written the crucial software for the new GUI over the weekend. He had been on a family camping trip when he wrote the required software using his laptop. This was great news!

The software-completion milestone for the new printer was met on time in the first week of December. Astonishingly, at the weekly project meeting, I was told again we had to drop the new GUI from the upcoming printer's features. The new obstacle was the time required for the quality-assurance (QA) engineer to thoroughly test the new GUI feature. She only had the following two weeks to complete the review of all possible color combinations in order to confirm that the correct colors were printed. Regrettably, there was only one QA engineer available and the evaluation work was estimated to require an additional two weeks due to the numerous color combinations to be tested.

Me: “I want to make sure I understand the situation. One of our best software engineers thought this new feature was important enough that he spent his family camping trip writing the software for it and now we can’t find enough QA resources to thoroughly test the new feature in time to meet the QA deadline?”

QA Manager: “That is correct.”

Me: “Does this QA testing basically consists of reviewing the printed images with the change instructions and confirming the correct colors are printed?”

QA Manager: “Yes.”

Me: “Okay, you provide the change instructions and the resulting images that need to be reviewed and I’ll have the instructions and final images compared. If any of the images are incorrect, I’ll let you know.”

QA Manager: “Tim, who in marketing has 80 available hours to work on this project during the next two weeks?”

Me: “I don’t have just one person to do the work; I have a team of marketing colleagues who will support me in this endeavor.”

That said, the team agreed to keep the new GUI feature in the upcoming printer release.

As it turned out, our QA team found the necessary personnel to test the new GUI without needing any marketing assistance. The printer was successfully launched on time and included the new GUI. Also, because the new GUI offered such a breakthrough for ease-of-use when it came to specifying colors, the printer was awarded the prestigious, *Printer of the Year* award by a printer trade magazine.

I came away from that project with two observations. First, when someone wants you to make a decision where none of the options are reasonable, try to buy time and wait to see if a better option appears on the horizon before the deadline. For example, there was no reason to cancel the new GUI in September when the engineering-completion milestone was three months away. Secondly, as I mentioned in an earlier story[10], requests should be used wisely. Because I hadn't made numerous requests in the past concerning insignificant issues, I had established a positive relationship with the development team and they agreed to delay the cancelation of the new GUI feature early in the printer development cycle. This delay gave our key engineer time to find an opportunity to write the necessary software for the new feature.

When should you make a tough decision that you do not want to make? Not until you absolutely must because a better option may appear tomorrow.

---

[10] See *Use Your Requests Wisely.*

Runaway Pup

One night many years ago I saw my neighbor Tommy trying to catch his new puppy that had slipped out of the backyard. It was a comical scene watching Tommy chase the puppy while it ran just fast enough to stay out of reach. It just so happened I realized my shoe was untied so I knelt down to tie it. Seeing me kneeling near the ground, the puppy became curious and dashed up to me which gave me the opportunity to grab his collar and hold him until Tommy could hook a leash onto the pup's collar and take him home.

Since that evening I have caught several other runaway puppies using that same technique. In fact, it happened just recently. I was out for an early evening walk when a young, black Labrador Retriever came from behind and sprinted past me. I looked back for the pup's owner and saw no one. When this type of incident occurred in the past, the owner was readily available. Unfortunately, this time the owner was nowhere in sight. The pup had obviously slipped out of its yard unbeknownst to the owner. Since the owner wasn't present, I hesitated trying to catch the pup. Yet after watching the pup dart back and forth between cars on the busy street, I decided it was too precarious of a situation. I knelt down on one knee and called to the pup. Upon hearing my voice and seeing me kneeling close to the ground, the pup came running over to me. I quickly snagged its collar and tried to read its dog tags for a phone number. The pup; however, thought I wanted to play and jumped up and began licking my face causing my glasses to fall off. Restoring my glasses and holding the pup's collar with one hand, I awkwardly called the number listed on one of the two dog tags. Unfortunately, the phone number was for the shelter where the pup was purchased and the shelter was closed. The second dog tag contained two additional phone numbers. My second call yielded no answer, as well as no voicemail prompt. Luckily, the third call was answered by a voicemail prompt which allowed me to leave a message. About 30 seconds later my phone rang just as the pup broke free and ran away. I told the pup's owner my location and that his pup had just slipped away. He said his daughter was on her way and thanked me for the call. With heavy traffic still on the road, I decided to try my trick again. Kneeling down once more, I called to the pup. Upon hearing my voice and seeing me low to the ground, it came running back. I quickly grabbed its collar and held it until a young girl ran up with a leash and took the pup home.

I slept well that night knowing the pup was safe with its family. If your pup ever slips away from you, don't chase it. Instead, kneel down close to the ground and call to it. I'll give you ten-to-one odds your pup will come running back to you.

The Wake

I normally don't attend a wake or a funeral unless I was well acquainted with the deceased; hence, it was unusual for me to attend Donna's wake. I hardly knew her; in fact, she probably didn't even know my name. Sadly, I anticipated that not too many people would be attending her service. I felt compelled to be present in order to support those who loved her and were going to miss her dearly.

My estimate about the number of attendees was correct. There were a dozen people present. Donna was a middle-aged women diagnosed with stage-four cancer. She bravely fought the illness for six months before succumbing to the inevitable. A few of Donna's close friends took turns standing up and speaking about her kindness and how she didn't deserve to die so young. It became quiet, very quiet. Everyone sat there not knowing what else to say or do, then Teresa spoke. She didn't stand to speak, but instead spoke while sitting in her chair:

> "Donna didn't like me! She didn't like me at all, not one bit! (pause) But last year when I got sick and I had no one to take care of me, Donna took me in. She gave me a place to sleep with blankets to keep me warm and she shared her

food with me. Donna nursed me back to health and if it hadn't been for her kindness, I wouldn't be here today."

Donna truly demonstrated a generous act of charity by taking Teresa into her home and nursing her back to health, especially since they weren't friends. Even more revealing about Donna's nature was that her home was very small. She didn't have an extra bedroom in the back of the house where she could isolate Teresa. In fact, Donna's home had only one room and the walls were not made of wood or bricks, but nylon. Donna's home was a tent and she was one of our community's homeless population.

When my time comes, I don't know whether I'll even get to see the gates of heaven, let alone pass through them. However, I am pretty sure about one thing; when Donna approached those gates, she was greeted by a host of angels who welcomed her as if she was their long-lost friend.

Reading the Circumstances

I recently went on a business trip with a few colleagues to a sales meeting. After arriving at our destination airport, we were waiting outside for the car rental van when I noticed a woman exiting the terminal. She was following a skycap and her arms were loaded with five, small, gift-wrapped packages. To both the woman's and my astonishment, the skycap stopped, released her rolling suitcase and said, "The van to your car rental facility should be here any minute." He abruptly turned and walked back into the terminal leaving the woman standing there with her arms full of packages and a desperate look on her face. It didn't require supernatural powers to know what was running through this woman's mind. She was obviously thinking, "How in the world am I going to pull my suitcase to a van when I have my arms full of these packages?" I immediately left my suitcase with a colleague and walked over to the women with the packages.

Me: "Can I help you with your suitcase?" The women looked at me as if I was speaking in a foreign language. I repeated my question, "Can I help you with your suitcase?"

Women: "Yes, yes, that would be wonderful!"

Me: "Which car rental company are you using today?"

Women: “Avis.”

I glanced down the long line of car rental vans that were parked next to the curb and noticed the Avis van had just pulled in behind the other vans.

Me: “Ah, your car rental van just arrived.” I took ahold of the woman’s suitcase handle and walked with her to the van.

Women: “Are you an angel?”

Me: “No ma’am.”

Woman: “Are you sure? You seem like an angel to me.”

Me: “Well thank you, but I have had a slew of past teachers who will attest to the fact that I’m no angel.” She laughed.

After loading her suitcase into the van and wishing her a safe journey, I returned to my colleagues who had loaded their suitcases along with mine into our car rental van. As I boarded the van, one of my friends asked, “Did she give you a tip?” I responded, “No, but she blessed me.” They laughed.

Many times, you don’t have to be able to read a person’s mind to know what he/she is thinking. All you have to do is look at the expression on their face and take note of their surrounding circumstances.

The Lost Cell Phone

My most recent job was working as a contract technical writer for a high-tech corporation. I was based in a large one-story warehouse which held over a hundred customer engineers and managers from different companies. Their jobs were to maintain the equipment which their companies had sold to a common customer.

Every morning when I arrived, I encountered a janitor whom I greeted with, “Good Morning.” He would smile, nod his head as if he understood me, but say nothing. After working for about a month, I heard him speaking Spanish to another employee and realized why he had never verbally responded to my greeting.

A couple of months later, the janitor walked into my cubical and handed me a cell phone. He then pointed at the Men’s room and shrugged his shoulders as if to say, “Beats me who owns this phone.” I found it ironic that of all the people who worked in that facility, the janitor chose me as the best person to find the phone’s owner, especially since I wasn’t a manager nor a permanent employee and I was probably the most recently person hired. Nevertheless, I accepted this daunting task by saying, “I’ll find the owner. Gracias!” I then gave him the thumbs-up sign to let him know that he had brought the phone to the correct person. He smiled, waved his hand and went back to work.

I initially considered waiting to see if the phone's owner would use another phone to try to call the lost phone, but I decided instead to be proactive. I went to one of my company's administrative assistants and asked, "Is there a Lost & Found department in this facility?"

She responded, "No, what did you lose?"

Me: "I didn't lose anything, but the janitor found this phone in the Men's room and gave it to me assuming I could find the phone's owner."

Assistant: "Is there a picture on the screen?"

Me: "Hmm, let me check."

I tapped the home button and an image appeared of a young man standing in a boat holding a large salmon. I didn't recognize the man so I handed the phone to the assistant and said, "Do you recognize this guy?"

Assistant: "Yes."

Me: "Does he work for our company?"

Assistant: "No, but I know where he sits. I can show you."

As we neared the far end of the building, I could see a young man in a cubical looking frustrated as he searched frantically for something. The assistant walked up to the man, handed him the phone and said, "Are you looking for this?"

He replied, "Yes! Thank you! Where did you find it?"

Assistant: "The janitor found it in the Men's room. Have a nice day."

As we walked back to our side of the building I said, "I think you just made yourself a new friend." She replied, "Maybe" and winked.

I thanked the assistant for her help and later that day when I saw the janitor, I told him the phone's owner had been found. He smiled, nodded his head and gave me the thumbs-up gesture as I had signaled to him earlier that day.

There are more sophisticated high-tech methods for finding a lost cell phone than just having your photo displayed on its screen, but it's a cheap and simple method to help your lost phone find its way back to you.

More importantly, being kind to people you don't know or who speak a different language can provide benefits not only to yourself, but to others.

Imaginary Baseball

Recently Lori and I went to a park with one of our daughters and her family. It was a fairly cold morning such that there were very few people present. My grandson played on the swings, monkey bars, jungle gym and ran from one climbing contraption to another until he became bored. That's when I strolled over to the vacant baseball field and called to him, "Do you want to play ball?"

Grandson: "Sure! Did you bring a bat and ball?"

Me: "Nope, we don't need them. Just go over to home plate and I'll pitch you an imaginary ball."

My grandson looked at me like I had lost my mind, but he proceeded to stroll over to home base.

Me: "When I pitch my imaginary ball to you, hit it as hard as you can with your imaginary bat and run to first base before I field the ball and tag you out. Got it?

Grandson: "Okay."

I wound my arm up and pitched the imaginary baseball. My grandson swung his imaginary bat, hit the imaginary ball and raced to first base as I fielded the ball and ran toward first base in my feeble attempt to tag him.

My wife called out, “He’s safe!”

Me: “Okay, Grandma, it’s your turn to bat.”

Lori stepped up to the plate. I pitched the imaginary ball again which she pretended to bunt and then ran to first base while I raced toward home to pick up the ball. I was not in time. She reached first base and my grandson reached second. I heard my daughter (who had walked over to home plate) say, “Okay Grandpa, let’s see what you’ve got.”

I wound up and pitched the ball which I pretended she clobbered. I ran into right field to pick up the ball. My grandson had reached third base and stopped, but Grandma yelled, “Run! Run Home!” He took off for home and I ran as fast as I could towards home, but my grandson scored!

There is only one rule when I play games with my grandchildren. They always win!

My Most Unforgettable Character

After living and working in Michigan for the last twenty years of his career, my Grandpa Kellogg retired and moved to Florida. Initially, he spent his days fishing in the ocean from a pier, but within a year, he became well known for his fishing skills such that some of the well-to-do retirees asked him to come out to sea on their yachts and teach them how to fish.

One day when Grandpa was fishing on a yacht, the motor died and the yacht began drifting toward a reef that was near shore. They immediately dropped the anchor to stop the yacht from colliding into the reef which could have caused severe damage. I should note that cell phones did not exist at that time. In fact, this yacht didn't even have a ship-to-shore radio. Because of the dire situation, Grandpa removed his shirt, shoes, socks and hat. He climbed into the ocean while wearing only his shorts and swam over the reef to the sandy beach where he proceeded to walk to a local bar. Using a pay phone, Grandpa called the Coast Guard and requested a ship be sent out to tow the yacht back to the marina. The local bartender must have been listening to the phone conversation because after Grandpa hung up, the bartender handed him a cold beer and said, "It sounds like you're having a rough day. How about a free beer?" Grandpa accepted the beer and thanked the bartender. Fortunately, the Coast Guard arrived before the yacht was damaged and towed it back to the marina. The amazing part about this story is Grandpa, who was over seventy years old at the time, had no problem climbing into the ocean, swimming across the reef and walking to the local bar to call the Coast Guard while wearing only his shorts! My only hope is that I'll be as fearless and agile should such a challenge occur for me at that age.

My grandparents didn't have a lot of money; therefore, after they moved to Florida, they only returned to Michigan once every two or three years. Upon their arrival, my family and I would meet them at the airport. One of the things I remember most about Grandpa was a facial line that started at the outside corner of his eye and ran down the side of his face. I loved that line; it's how I could easily identify him when we picked him up at the airport after not seeing him for so long.

Looking back, some of the best experiences I had in my youth were with my grandpa when he took my brother, a friend and me fishing on lakes like Sherman, Wall, Fine or Beadle. Grandpa would rent a row boat and while rowing us around the lake he would impart wild tales of his youth. Tales such as when he used to ride the paddlewheel boats up and down the Mississippi River and travel from town-to-town. Whenever he ran out of money, his cigar-maker union card would allow him to easily find work and upon filling his pockets with silver dollars, he would move onto another town. His years of wandering continued until he turned twenty-six when he met Willa Hiles, a petite woman with bright brown eyes and a warm smile. Upon marrying Willa, Grandpa's years of wandering came to an end. He settled down and began raising his family.

Those days I spent fishing with Grandpa were the most tranquil times I remember during my childhood. My goal is to bestow similar experiences with my grandchildren.

I now have a line starting at the outside corner of my eye just like Grandpa's. With each year, the line grows a little longer down the side of my face. I like this because it reminds me of Grandpa and I regard it as warriors regard their battle scars—with pride. After all, this line, along with all my other facial lines, represent the challenges I have faced and a lifetime of experiences. If these lines are any indication that I'm like Grandpa, then it makes me proud.

Appendix

Collegiate Wrestling Terms and Definitions

The following table provides a list of standard collegiate wrestling terms and their definitions.

Term	Definition
Escape	Wrestler A is on the mat. Wrestler B is on top of wrestler A and in control of wrestler A. When wrestler A breaks away from wrestler B, such that wrestler B is no longer in control of wrestler A and both wrestlers are back to the neutral position, then wrestler A has escaped and is awarded one point. An example of an escape move is the standup.
Fall/Pin	Wrestler A is on top of wrestler B and wrestler B's shoulder are held to the mat for two consecutive seconds. In such a scenario, wrestler A is said to have pinned wrestler B; and thereby, wrestler A has won the match.
Near Fall	Wrestler A has wrestler B on his back, such that: • When both of wrestler B's shoulders are held within four inches of the mat, but not on the mat for a two-count then wrestler A is awarded two points for a near fall. However, if wrestler

Term	Definition
Near Fall (continued)	A is held for a four-count then wrestler B is awarded four points. • If one of wrestler B's shoulder touches the mat and the other shoulder is at a 45° angle coming down to the mat then wrestler A is awarded two points for a near fall. Examples of pinning combinations used to score near-fall points are over-the-top cradle, half-nelson, guillotine and banana split.
Referee's Position	Wrestler A starts with his/her hands and knees down on the mat, and wrestler B starts on top, behind and in control of wrestler A. Both the second and third periods of a match start with the wrestlers in the referee's position.
Reversal	Given wrestler A is on the mat and wrestler B is on top of wrestler A. If wrestler A comes out from under wrestler B and gains control over wrestler B, such that wrestler A is on top of wrestler B, then wrestler A performed a reversal and is awarded two points. Examples of reversal moves are switch, standing switch and side roll.
Riding Styles	Wrestler A is said to be riding wrestler B when wrestler B is down on the mat and wrestler A is on top of wrestler B. There have been different

Term	Definition
Riding Styles (continued)	eras in the sport of wrestling when at the end of a match a point has been awarded to the wrestler who had more than one minute of riding time than his/her opponent's riding time. Examples of riding styles are near arm and far ankle, tight waist and near arm, standard leg riding and figure-four leg riding.
Takedown	When both wrestlers are on their feet and wrestler A takes wrestler B down to the mat and lands on top of wrestler B, such that wrestler A is in control of wrestler B, then wrestler A has scored a takedown and is awarded two points. Examples of takedowns are single leg, double leg, duck under and fireman carry.

About the Author

This is Tim Kellogg's debut title. He has worked as a construction laborer, 9th grade math teacher, high school wrestling coach, systems analyst, training manager, product marketing manager and technical writer. He grew up in Michigan and has since lived in Oklahoma, Ohio, Texas and now Oregon.

Tim has four grown children and six grandchildren to date and currently resides in Portland, Oregon with his wife Lori where they enjoy hiking and exploring the Great Northwest.

Made in the USA
Monee, IL
20 October 2023

44908873R00108